This paperback edition published in 2019 by

Little Toller Books
Ford, Pineapple Lane, Dorset

First published in 1948 by George Allen and Unwin

ISBN 978-1-908213-70-9

Text and photographs © The Estate of Walter Murray 2018

Introduction © Raynor Winn 2019

We have made every effort to contact the Estate of Walter Murray;
please notify Little Toller Books with further information
as regards the copyright-holders.

Typeset in Sabon by Little Toller Books
Printed in Cornwall, UK by TJ Books

All papers used by Little Toller Books
are natural, recyclable products made from
wood grown in sustainable, well-managed forests

A CIP catalogue record for this book is available
from the British Library

3 5 7 9 8 6 4

Copsford

by Walter J. C. Murray

LITTLE TOLLER BOOKS

CONTENTS

INTRODUCTION

Raynor Winn

Alone in the darkness of a derelict cottage defending his bed against an army of rats was not what Walter John Campbell Murray had in mind when he moved to the country. His escape to a rural idyll led him to Copsford, a ruined house a mile from the nearest habitation, where the wind rushed up the stairs and water poured through the roof. But the year he spent in the Sussex countryside, immersed in the plants and wildlife of postwar England, was to change his life. When, many years later, he finally wrote of his experiences at Copsford, it was a story of his discovery of a spiritual connection to nature. His writing has been compared to the more widely known Richard Jefferies, but his concern for nature and the environment made him a forerunner of modern writers, such as Roger Deakin and Robert Macfarlane.

Like many in their early twenties, Murray was eager for adventure and wider horizons. He needed to find what life had to offer beyond the limits of his rural family home. Born in 1900, Murray had been too young to endure much of the hardships of the First World War. He joined the Merchant Navy but quickly found he didn't like the sea, so with his feet back on dry land he joined the RAF with the hope of taking to the skies. Luckily for him, the war ended before he learnt how to fly and he returned to his home village of Horam in Sussex unscathed by war. Still carrying the joy and hope for life that had been stripped from many of his peers, he packed his bag with a few meagre belongings and left the countryside of his youth to explore the possibilities of London and a job in journalism.

Murray had a lot to learn, but unexpectedly his discoveries were mainly about himself. Journalism proved to consist of dull, uninspiring reports, offering little of the glamour and excitement he had imagined. His accommodation was equally miserable: 'that third-floor-back with its tiny gas fire, its naked electric light and its distressing view'. Very soon he was finding no inspiration in the city, instead he longed for 'solitude among woods and hills' where he could 'live close to nature'.

Devising a plan to live cheaply in the countryside by picking herbs to sell for medicinal purposes, Murray thought he could make enough money to survive. But that wasn't the real reason for his return to the country, nor was it, as he suggests, a desire to live a 'solitary life'; he was drawn by a far stronger force. In his early days at Copsford, reflecting on his time in London, he began to know that he was 'of the country'. With that realisation came the understanding of his own powerful connection to nature and how that drove his creativity; 'I could not dip my pen in the lifeblood of the city streets. I needed the very song of the shadow-dappled brook to write, with the sound of wild wings in my ears and the scent of wildflowers in my nostrils.'

Anyone who has dreamt of spending time alone in the natural environment will connect with Murray's emotions during the first weeks after his arrival at Copsford. Much as he had craved being alone, the sense of isolation he felt when he entered the house oppressed him; 'the loneliness of the place repelled me, repelled me forcibly.' The sense of emptiness in the house that had been uninhabited for years was overwhelming. Out in nature, his solitude was all he had hoped for but within those walls, where humans should dwell, he felt his solitude most acutely, unable to sleep upstairs because he felt 'cut off from the front door'. But he wasn't alone; very quickly he found he was sharing the house with an army of rats. As he began a territorial battle with them, the silence of the house was lost and he began to find comfort in the ramshackle shelter it represented.

With so much time to spare, Murray describes how he 'learnt to be still'. Although his days involved the picking and drying of herbs, they also contained hours of emptiness. He writes of his 'inborn love of the countryside' being the reason for him being able to overcome the 'discontent' provoked by those empty hours. *Copsford* isn't written with a deep exploration of emotion as seen in many modern works, but in these spaces between Walter's busy activities we can see how he was being transformed, gaining a far deeper connection to his environment and just occasionally catching a 'glimpse of the intricate and complex pattern of life'.

His vicarage upbringing in a small rural community before the First World War had been repressive in many ways, but time spent alone and the need to wash began to peel away that inhibition. His childhood attraction to 'wild and unconventional water' had been controlled by convention, but at Copsford Murray cast his clothes aside and plunged into a pool of wild water. He talks of this as being an 'outward sign of my inward awareness of at-one-ment'. In a book that describes his many 'wonders and delights', this was clearly his greatest.

As the summer passed and slipped into autumn, Murray began to feel a deeper connection to nature: 'it was closer contact than touch, it was almost union'. Discussing this connection in *The Green Man of Horam*, his biographer Tom Wareham describes Murray as a 'nature mystic'. The story of his herbs and the land from which he gathered them went deeper than a simple portrait of his country life, as he pondered the 'prodigality which scatters beauty with so lavish a hand everywhere around us'. In *Copsford* Murray takes a questioning approach, balancing nature observations with science, and suggesting time is the resolution to his struggle between science and religion: 'What is time in the evolution of an idea and its expression in life?' In *Nature's Undiscovered Kingdom*, a collection of essays written before *Copsford*, Murray had already explored this 'lavish hand'; 'life, the vital element, spirit mind, God, if you will', as if saying – there is a force, but you call it whatever you choose. Murray's dilemma as he tries to find a hand behind natural beauty led him to suggest it is 'God's idea' talking about the 'Artist' and 'Creator'. Wareham's summing up of this struggle probably best describes Murray's feelings: 'it is almost as if he is saying, "Call it God if you want to, but it is not quite what I have in mind".'

Copsford has an innocence, a freedom in thought and life that is less present in his other books. Written in the 1940s, two decades after the last bunch of herbs was sent to the market, Murray's recollections of this time are as clear as if they had been written only a year or two after. Undoubtedly his experiences alone in the Sussex countryside profoundly influenced the rest of his life; the joy, almost ecstasy, that he describes stayed with him through his career as a teacher and in his nature conservation work and writing. Yet it was written very shortly after the death of his only son, Dick, at the age of fifteen. He does not write of his personal tragedy and barely touches on his own emotions outside of his nature connections, but it is hard not to think that as Murray sat down to write about the young Walter, that Dick was ever present in his thoughts. His later work, *A Sanctuary Planted*, is regarded as part eulogy to his son and gives a more Christian resolution to his questioning. But *Copsford* captures the spirit of his youth, his nature spirit. As Murray imagined his younger self living free in a natural wonderland, perceiving 'meaning instead of things' and living as 'a part of all creation', his son must have been an influence. Yet only once does he mention death, when he remembers a tiny copper butterfly that had become extinct. In thoughts that predate the modern conservation movement, years ahead of his time, he talks about changing climate and physical conditions, and yet something of the shadow of Dick is in what he says: 'What else is there so tragic as the loss of a life form that can never, never reappear. I know it has happened hundreds, more probably thousands of times in the past; creatures have, as it were, taken the wrong turning, to find themselves in a blind alley from which there is no retreat only extinction. Changing climate and conditions have, slowly or suddenly, wiped out legions of living creatures as completely and with the finality as I rub chalk figures from the slate that records my agrimony tally. The dust blows out of the open door.' In reimaging his own youth, possibly in some way he was giving Dick the youth he didn't have, giving him back the life that had 'blown out of the open door'.

As the rain pours through the open roof of Copsford we have to cheer for the transformed Walter Murray, as he strips off his clothes and wades across the swollen river, away from the house for the last time, running downhill to his 'music mistress' and the start of his 'magic book of life'.

Raynor Winn
Polruan, Cornwall, 2019

ONE IN A MILLION

MOST OF US, I suppose, sooner or later in our lives, experience the desire to live alone, to have our own cabin, cottage, castle and be far from the madding crowd. There is a fascination about the faraway island across the glittering southern seas, about the mountaintop shrouded in heavy mists, about the quiet clearing in the heart of the forest, that few can resist. For some the urge comes but once in a lifetime, for others it is insistent.

While we are children the desert island idea appeals to us most strongly. The story of Crusoe never palls, although in our imagination the word desert only means deserted, and, for us, the island must be a paradise with every useful and lovely thing growing at the very door of our hut. We want the island of the Swiss Family Robinson, but at the same time we must be monarch of all we survey. We would live in a tree or a cave.

A few years older, and we have grown so accustomed to many of the comforts of civilised life that we would not do without them. We are still seized, quite often, with the desire to live alone, but now it must be a log cabin or comfortable cottage, with main water and electric light, and with a wireless set in the chimney corner.

Later still, after experiencing the rough-and-tumble of life, after strenuous affairs in business, or heartrending affairs in love, we long to be alone, and picture solitude among woods and hills in forgotten corners of the world, where we can live close to nature, and hear the beating of her heart and feel her soft and kindly touch.

None is born to solitude, not one in ten thousand achieves it, not one in a million has it thrust upon him.

When all unexpectedly I suddenly left the hive of London and discovered myself to be that solitary figure, that one in a million, probably one of London's many millions, I hardly knew whether to be glad or sorry. Suddenly to be thrust into solitude is like a nice cold drink from the depths of the well.

It was not that I was absolutely compelled to live a solitary life, but circumstances were such that if I was to seize the only opportunity that offered to escape from the misery of a third-floor-back off King's Street, SW1, then perforce I must find a cottage in the heart of the country; a cottage that cost next to nothing to rent, that had sufficient room for the work I had in mind, and above all, a cottage which had the open, flower-filled countryside at its very doors.

Could such a place be found? On the face of it, it was out of the question; such desirable country cottages are more in demand and higher in rent than country mansions. But sometimes it happens that while the countryside is indeed at the very doors, nothing else happens to be. The demand for that cottage is in inverse proportion to the square of the distance between it and the ordinary services and comforts of civilised life. If it lies at a great distance, there is no demand for it at all.

I had known of such a place; no one had wanted it for twenty years. The open country surrounded it like the southern ocean about a coral island. But was it to let? A friend, who lived in the village, ascertained that at least it was still empty, though her report that it was derelict did not sound encouraging. However, I burned my boats behind me, left forever that third-floor-back with its tiny gas fire, its naked electric light and its distressing view, turned my back on London and sped away to the village street, there to reconnoitre and perhaps negotiate.

The owner, upon whose land the cottage stood, was an energetic, tireless, one-man farmer. He was a stockily built little fellow, with curly, grizzly hair and a weather-beaten, rosy face. He had a habit of tilting his hat over his eyes and scratching the back of his head whenever anything outside the rut of farm life puzzled or worried him. He was much perplexed, then, when I first asked him about the cottage. He simply could not understand it all. Why anyone in their senses should want to take that place beat him. 'Why, it's sech a mile from nowhere,' he kept repeating. I said I did not mind about that, it was rather what I wanted.

He looked at me doubtfully, and picking a long bent, began methodically to chew it.

'There ain't no water, and there ain't no drainage neither,' he said.

I was impressed, but not abashed. 'I can fetch and carry my drinking water,' I replied.

The hat was now at such a forward angle that he had to bend his head backwards to look at me, and the bent and the brim touched in front of his nose. He was very much puzzled. I could see, too, that he felt that he would be responsible for all the privations and hardships of a tenant. He would like to let the cottage, of course, and pocket an odd shilling or two a week, but he felt in duty bound to prevent anyone from being such a fool as to go and live in the place.

'No one ain't lived in Copsford for more 'an twenty years,' he protested. 'It do be out of repair like.'

I said that I could understand that, but perhaps it would suit my purpose nevertheless.

'You'm best go an' 'ave a look round first,' he suggested. Then returning to the familiar rut, 'I be goin' ploughin' in the ten-acre.'

He readjusted his hat and began to harness his two horses. He was happy again, so I set off across the field to inspect Copsford, this cottage 'sech a mile from nowhere' where no one wanted to live.

To be a mile from anywhere may not seem to account for impressive or repellent isolation. But Copsford was peculiarly situated, and the mile referred to so frequently by the farmer was the distance of the cottage to the nearest lane, as the heron flies. In other directions tracks and roads were still farther away. The nearest inhabited dwelling was the farmer's own cottage which was close to the lane-side; other farms and houses were some way beyond that. The village was hidden from view two

miles away. No road or cart track or any sort of footpath led through
the fields and woods towards Copsford. There had been rough tracks
in the past, but nothing recognisable remained except here and there
grass-covered or hedge-filled depressions. These I only found and traced
many months later.

Copsford stood just back from the summit of a low, round hill. About
the base of the hill, like the moat of a fortress, a brook meandered, and
with a tributary, cut off the cottage from neighbouring territory on three
sides. The brook, known as the Darn, was just too wide and generally too
deep to be easily crossed. It was fringed with alders, hazels and hawthorn,
and it helped very much in the isolation of Copsford. It always looked to
me as though the narrow, flat-bottomed marshy valleys, along the edges
of which the Darn and its tributary flowed, had once been the beds of
much greater rivers, which in times gone by had joined in a mad whirl
below the hill and completely isolated the cottage. Many months later I
had good cause to believe there was much truth in my surmise.

There was one bridge over the brook, but when I reached it I was
surprised to find it heavily fenced on both sides. It was as awkward
to cross as the brook itself, and when over, I felt I had passed much
more than a brook. I seemed to have crossed a frontier, or to have burst
through some intangible screen which shrouded the little hill and veiled
the mystery of the unwanted cottage.

There was something, too, about the countryside that was different.
It seemed wilder and desolate, inhospitable. I could not explain it then;
I just sensed a change that was forbidding; and this was not altogether
imagination, as afterwards I found real causes for the impression I received.

Furthermore, the fact that the cottage stood at the summit of the
hill increased its loneliness. For when anyone ever did pass the brook
and wander into the deserted countryside beyond, the hill pushed their
footsteps aside. There was no purpose in climbing the hill; it was far
easier going and more interesting along the banks of the brook. Besides
this, the stray trespasser would naturally prefer to avoid a cottage. Thus
only those who had legitimate business at Copsford would mount the

hill, and so the place was left alone, terribly alone.

On that side of the hill not bounded by the brook were one or two very rough pastures and unkempt copses, and these were again hemmed in by an extensive wood: Darn Wood. Old John Guy, the oldest inhabitant of the village, who had known this empty countryside as well as his kitchen garden, told me afterwards that Darn or Dern meant a lonely place. He knew all there was to know about the wood and the brook and the hilltop. He knew Copsford when it had been a little farmstead with a barn or two, and stables, with byre and sty. He had seen smoke rise from its chimneys and had smelt the straw in its rickyard.

But I am digressing. I was a solitary figure toiling up the hill to catch my first glimpse of Copsford. There were no barns, no ricks, and there was no smoke mounting from its stark chimney.

THE COTTAGE

I SHALL NEVER FORGET the first time I mounted the hill. It was a dull day in middle spring, and a strong southwesterly wind blew in my face as I toiled upwards towards the cottage. The wind had that cool, penetrating edge that for certain promises rain, and from horizon to horizon the sky was monotonously grey. Conditions would not have been happy for inspecting the ideal home, but for Copsford, well, at the time they were indeed dreary; nothing could have been sadder or added more to the intense loneliness of the place. Yet looking back I would not have had it otherwise; Copsford could not have been wooed gilded in sunshine and haloed in cirrus blue.

It was characteristic of the place that I heard it before I saw it. As I approached, the blustering wind brought to my ears the forlorn rattle of ill-fitting windows that had not been opened for twenty years. There was, too, the thump-thump of a door that swung heavily but never latched. And then I saw it. Grass grew up to the very door step. The walls were bare, hideously bare; no ivy, rambler, not a plant or shrub nestled against them; just stark brick from grey slate roof to the ground. It would not have been Copsford had bowers of honeysuckle overhung the porch or sweet clematis smiled about the sills. There were four windows and a door, not in the usual childish arrangement, but three on the upper floor, and one on the ground floor to the left of the front door. They were square-cornered and grim, and several broken panes gaped darkly at me. There was an ugly grey chimney-stack at the southend. The cottage faced east, and on the north wall was a half-ruined brick-and-slate shed, the door to which was gone. There had been a wood fence between what should have been the garden and the field, but only the uprights remained and one or two tumbled crossbars, crumbling in their slots. The rough grass of the field swept in unhindered, lapped the walls of the cottage, washed round behind it. Like a flood-tide it swamped everything; the cottage stood, a barren, inhospitable rock in the midst.

When at last I stood before the house I could not at first find courage to push the blistered door and write my name on this forgotten page of life. The loneliness of the place repelled me, repelled me forcibly, and I would have left it gladly in peace and for ever had I not needed just such a place. So I shook the cold hand from my shoulder and, pushing open the unlatched door, stepped over the threshold.

I found myself in what had evidently been the living room. An old-fashioned kitchen range tottered half in and half out of the fireplace. There was no hearthstone; instead there was a great hole in the floor choked with soot, crumbling mortar and broken bricks. There were two windows. The larger one I had already seen from outside beside the door; the other, smaller, one was on the right-hand side of the chimney and faced south. Both frames were loose at the sill, and the sash cords had long since rotted. The panes that were unbroken were so curtained with cobweb and grime that they let little light in, and the room was darkened in consequence. The cracked ceiling was neither white nor black, and here and there the dirty damp-stained walls boasted a few square feet of discoloured and peeling wallpaper. Between the skirting and the floor I counted some half-dozen rat-holes, and in addition I noticed a big hole in the lower panel of the front door, evidently the rats' front entrance also. The floor was thick with their filth and the whole atmosphere of the place reeked of these vermin.

Thinking that I heard a movement overhead, I paused in the midst of my dust-raising investigations and listened. And then in an instant the chill loneliness of the place swooped down upon me; the cold hand that had rested upon my shoulder now clutched me violently by the throat and the appalling dreariness which so many years' solitude had fashioned, held me motionless. Those few seconds of my life are graven so deep in my memory that I think nothing can ever efface them, yet they are altogether indescribable. It was as though the place resented intrusion, as though human life had no further right there. It resisted passively while I moved and made a noise, but the moment I stood still it reasserted its own character with an intensity that was appalling. Its grip was icy. I was frozen motionless, numbed in heart and mind.

The forlorn tattoo of the windows upstairs echoed fitfully about the house. The wind throbbed in the great chimney, and, pouring in through the broken panes, made the peeling paper titter and rasp along the walls. The door slammed to with a violent thump behind me and the room darkened suddenly with its closing. Scarcely had its startling echoes died away than, listening as I have never listened before, I heard a scampering sound overhead, a scampering which grew louder, a violent crescendo of hurrying multitudes, a crash followed by showers of plaster as though a ton of rubble had fallen from roof to floor within the walls, and then stillness. A stillness more terrifying than any movement, and only the wind moaned in the chimney and the wallpaper jittered along the walls.

Often after a hideous dream, when suddenly we wake filled with a dread of we know not what, we dare not move and scarce dare breathe, even though we are in the comfort of our own beds with familiar objects on every side. It requires an effort to re-enter our normal waking life. Something of the same paralysis gripped me as I stood there for the first time within Copsford. I suppose it was only for a few seconds, but it might have been many hours. It required a great effort even to breathe and a concentration of willpower to relax those muscles which held me as rigid as a dead stick.

Then suddenly the tension snapped. I stamped, I shouted, I hove a brick at random, rumbling along the floorboards and crack against the skirting. The cottage re-echoed with the din. I slammed cupboards, I banged doors, and when at length I desisted and again forced myself to listen, I was immediately conscious that the spell was broken, anyway for the time being, and that I could move and breathe about the house without suffering suffocation from sheer loneliness.

A parallel to this strange experience I found in an unusual tale of the

Antarctic. When I read it and by whom it was written I simply cannot remember, or I would gladly acknowledge it. It concerned three twentieth-century seamen who discovered a derelict in those remote polar seas. By her build they knew her to be many centuries old. She was just a mastless hull rolling in the trough. Not without some hesitation they boarded her, and when at length they succeeded in uncovering and unfastening one of the hatches and peered down into the cabin there disclosed, they saw to their amazement that everything therein was completely undisturbed. Even the glasses and cutlery stood arranged upon the table. The most venturesome of the three determined to lower himself into the cabin and discover the secret of this weird immobility. But the moment he lowered his legs below the hatch and dropped on to the table the other two sailors, to their horror, saw their shipmate's trousers thrust up his legs, as if by invisible hands. Panic seized the venturesome sailor, who vainly endeavoured to haul himself up again. But even as the other two leaned over to grasp him, he lost his balance, and staggering drunkenly, tottered sideways and fell from the table. With bulging eyes and mouth agape he lay on his back dead – suffocated.

The storyteller explains that the air in the long-closed cabin had somehow or other become solid like a jelly, and that it was not until the two wretched sailors had hacked and slashed it to pieces, and hurled the horrible, transparent substance overboard that they were able to enter the cabin safely.

So it seemed with Copsford. It was not until I had rent and slashed that suffocating solitude and silence with the noise of human speech and endeavour that I could begin to move about without being overwhelmed by its oppressive loneliness. My shouts, my stamping, my banging of doors filled the house with familiar sounds which had, no doubt, resounded from the walls years ago, and so, for the moment at any rate, it accepted me. Incidentally the noises which were familiar to me and to the cottage of long ago were certainly unfamiliar to the rats. My din seemed to have struck terror into ratland, and no more wild scampering disturbed me. I continued my investigations. The living room, which was the full width of the cottage, was comparatively large, being about twelve feet square. Immediately adjoining it on the right was a small brick-floored scullery. There was a rough grey stone sink under the window, which faced north, and both sink and window were indescribably filthy. In the corner was a hollow of crumbling, soot-grimed bricks – it had been the copper. Winding abruptly out of the further corner of this chill scullery twisted the wooden stairs. They were not open stairs with a banister, but were, so to speak, within the wall, and furthermore there was a door to them. When the door was shut no staircase was visible. Although I have lived in the country for three-quarters of my life, I had never lived in a house in which there was a door to the stairs. I know now that it is common enough in many old cottages, and recently has been advertised as quite a feature in modern dwellings, but when I went to Copsford it was new and strange to me. It suggested that at one time the occupants of the cottage had sought security above – security from what? I shall never know; perhaps from nothing more unpleasant than the steam of the week's washing. I could never have slept upstairs feeling cut off from the front door; even to have it closed during daylight hours was uncomfortable, so I never touched it. In fact, like most doors in the cottage, it was warped and would not latch, and there were rat-holes in it. I propped it firmly open with several bricks and went upstairs.

There was a tiny landing, about a yard square, lit by a window still smaller. The window was the only one in the house that looked towards the west, that is, out at the back. Through its cobwebs and grime I could see trees and the little tangled wilderness of what should have been the back garden. Three doors, shoulder to shoulder, led off the landing. I entered the room opposite the head of the stairs. It had a largish window and a fireplace, and after what I had seen below appeared brighter and cleaner. This may have been because the window was open, the upper sash being jammed level with the lower. Birds had taken full advantage of this and droppings and feathers littered the floor. Rats, too, had liked this room, for I counted no fewer than fifteen holes in the floor and the skirting, some large enough to lose a five-shilling piece down. I never could understand why the rats had worked so desperately hard and made so many entrances into one room. Perhaps they were emergency exits, making safe the sudden departure of many, but I must not anticipate my adventure with the rats. That came later.

Neither of the other rooms was at all attractive. One was very small, about five feet by seven, the other dark and angular, with its floor inches deep in litter, which might have been old oats and clover seed. I could not bring myself to walk on this uncertain carpet; I dreaded what might spring from it – the last straw broke the camel's back! So I stealthily closed the door and crept downstairs and out into the open air.

Very pleasant it was, after the grime and mustiness of the rat-ridden cottage, to lean into the strong wind and face away southwards to the distant line of grey Downs, and to fill my lungs with the pure air. A peewit drove up against the gale, and tumbling at sight of me, whirled over the hedge like a blown leaf. There was rain in the wind now, and the sky was as grey and sad as ever, yet there was something magical in this lonely countryside with its rough pastures, its unkempt hedges, snowy with ragged blackthorn, its woodlands hazy green, its winding brooks. But Copsford was so altogether impossible with its broken panes and falling plaster, its useless stove, its legion of rats. Could I ever live there? I remembered the third-floor-back with every modern convenience and its appalling view of roofs and chimneys and slum yards, and I groaned. A house agent once told me that almost invariably the first thing his clients do when he shows them a house for sale is to walk straight to the window of the first room they inspect to see the view, and if the view is worth the seeing the house is as good as sold, no matter if the roof leaks or you can push your thumb-nail into the window frames.

As I looked at the view from the top of the hill I thought of summer days. Through the grey curtains of rain that were now drawing across the wooded landscape I saw in imagination summer blue, when all the shimmering countryside would be at my very door, when the lark would sing above my roof, and the snipe would bleat in the marsh. I saw the possibility of doing what it had often been my great desire to do, to live alone and at one with nature. The view was winning me over. In spite of the ghastly state of the cottage I began to think it might be cleaned, the rat-holes might be blocked and the rats destroyed; one room at least might be made habitable, other rooms could be used for the purpose I had in mind. As I thought, so my footsteps returned towards Copsford. I looked up and saw it staring bleakly at me, and bodily motion and wishful thinking both halted abruptly – impossible! But as I stared, a pair of partridges sprang suddenly from the grass at the very door of the cottage. It was enough; I would take Copsford.

It only remained for me to return to the lane-side and arrange it with the farmer. I would not enter the cottage again; I would not even look at it, for I knew well enough that another glimpse of its rat-riddled desolation would too easily weigh down the balance in favour of my leaving it for good. So I hastened away down the hill trying to close my ears to the shudder of the windows and the sullen boom of the door. The rain drove past me in ragged squalls and the way became sodden and slippery. I crossed the marsh and the foam-flecked Darn and came at length to civilised fields where the farmer followed the plough.

Twice the labouring horses came to my end of the furrows, and each time I let them go again without hailing the farmer. But the third time, as the straining team toiled up the field with manes blowing and backs streaming, and the little grizzled farmer plodding manfully behind, I was too forcibly reminded of those who put hands to the plough to vacillate any longer, so without more ado I walked to the end of the last neatly folded furrow, there to seal my fate.

With clanking of harness and churning of mud the plough came to rest, and as the farmer sat upon the handle I told him that I would rent Copsford. He must perforce tilt his hat and a stream of water poured from the brim, but he was too astonished to notice it. He had been quite certain that the place was uninhabitable. I told him that I thought it would suit my purpose quite well. 'Oh yes,' he said, scratching his back hair, and looking at me as though he thought I was not all there. 'I suppose you might tidy 'er a bit.'

I agreed with him, and suggested that perhaps he would remove the old oats and clover seed.

'They be no good now,' he replied, and I took it that he meant the stuff was not worth his removing. Next I asked him what the rent would be.

'I dunno, I dunno,' he pondered. 'It do be sech a mile from nowhere. Would three shillin's a week be hurtin' you?'

No, that was a very convenient sum! Then I must be sure that I had the right to wander anywhere I liked.

'Why o' course,' he agreed willingly enough. 'You don't want to be cooped up there, lonesome like it do be. Anywheres you like.'

This I was very grateful for, because I must have the run of the countryside for the work I proposed, though I felt a tremor when even this toil-stained one-man farmer mentioned the lonesomeness of the place. One last question: could I get my drinking water from him and buy milk at the farm?

'There be the well,' he said, standing up and resettling the hat. 'You dip what you want and 'twon't be much neither. The missus, she'll sell you milk, as much as ever you be wanting.'

'That's settled, then,' I said.

It was.

'Up Bess, up Nell; come on, come on there!'

Away goes the plough, and the Copsford agreement is signed and sealed in the good brown soil.

HOUSE CLEANING

WITH THE HELP of my friend the music teacher, who lived in the village, I procured broom, pail, soap and scrubbing-brush, and on Whit Monday morning set out across the fields for Copsford. At the farm I dipped in the well and filled my bucket, and while doing so saw the farmer's wife peeping behind the lace curtains. Well she might, for I was indeed an object of curiosity, a mine for gossip. But she was a grand old soul, and whatever she may have thought she never spoke, and later took quite a motherly interest in my comings and goings. She always had my milk, and often my water, waiting for me on the doorstep. But she never came to Copsford, no, nor ever crossed the Darn – that was none of her business.

It was a glorious day for my second visit to the cottage. One of those days which are like jewels among the many-coloured beads of spring. A day when we seem to breathe not air but sunshine, when the sky is high and deeply blue, the horizon faintly far, when the woods ring with the bird music and the new green is still so light that there seems more branch than leaf. A day when to live is joy, and a run, a leap and a dance in the sunshine would be the natural expression of our delight.

Encumbered as I was, it was difficult for me to restrain the impulse to run, and at last I could hold back no longer, but sped away down the slight incline to the brook with sufficient noise to set all marshland agog. Several things happened simultaneously. A green woodpecker – I could see his red head as he went – fled shrieking with laughter away towards Copsford, half a dozen moorhens scuttled with necks a-stretch for the brook, and with magnificent calm and lofty disdain, a heron spread his enormous wings and beat slowly up above the alders and disappeared in the sunshine downstream. Needless to say, I came to a standstill.

Such an unexpected glimpse of my future neighbours was more than I had expected, more in every way, and I could have whooped for joy. But it would have been a bad mistake to have begun my acquaintance among the wild folk with noisy terror. So I checked the shout and bowed to the noble heron, waved my broom at the mocking woodpecker, and walked more cautiously among the kingcups lest I should accidentally crush a baby moorhen and add murder to my reputation.

Thus I came to the little hill and for the second time approached Copsford. Although the brightness of the day did not make the cottage any the more hospitable, it took away the heart-crushing dreariness, and on swinging open the front door I was cheered by the sight of the sunshine pouring in through the broken panes and making jagged, gilded patterns in the dust. Remembering my first experience, I did not pause. I dropped the handle oft he pail with a clash, flung down broom and brushes, propped the door wide open with a couple of bricks, ran up and downstairs like a clod-hopper, and never for a moment paused to listen.

My first task was to open the windows and let in light and air, and more light and more air. The mustiness, the damp, the gloom must be shot to tatters. But the sash cords were rotted away and it was not easy. Windows in this condition are horribly unmanageable and dangerous. The top sash will often stay in position although the cords are gone: you think it is jammed or stiff and give it a tug, and without the slightest warning it will descend with a crash and the swiftness of the guillotine. I just saved my head, but the two bottom panes were shivered to splinters. I was more cautious with the others and propped them open with bits of board. The sashes were never repaired, first because no carpenter could afford the time and energy to trudge all that way with his bag of tools, and second because

I could not afford to have him spend so much time.

The next task was to sweep the house down. Probably you have not had the job of spring-cleaning a house twenty years untenanted, but perhaps you can imagine what a suffocating labour it was. Ceilings, walls, windows, floors were matted and festooned with cobwebs and rotting paper, mildew and mould, and the work and filth of generations of rats and mice. Five minutes' work with the broom created such a fog that I could neither see nor breathe. But I would not sprinkle water, for this only sticks the muck to the floor, and besides I hadn't the water to spare. In each of the three upstairs rooms I created the same commotion and soon had a huge pile of rubbish at the head of the stairs. It was bad house-cleaning no doubt, but without more ado I hove the whole lot downstairs whither it went like a cataract. But a great draught, which I have learnt to know well since, seized upon the dusty spray and whirled it up the tunnel of the stairs in a choking cloud. Blinded and gasping, I slammed the doors and fled into one of the rooms to get my breath and to wait till the dust storm subsided.

The tremendous uprush of air from the lower to the upper storey in the cottage, by way of the stairs, I never properly understood. Whether it was caused by the position of the building just below the summit of the hill, or whether an occasional characteristic of enclosed stairs, I cannot explain. It was not always present even on windy days; it seemed to be dependent on other causes. Perhaps the uneven heating of the cottage – it was always cold and dank below – had something to do with it. Summer or winter it might be expected, and here at least was one reason why there was a door at the foot of the stairs.

I worked hard with the broom and Copsford slowly became dean. Clean, that is, by comparison, for there remained much scrubbing and window-cleaning to be done. It was surprising how often one could go over the same bit of wall or the same patch of floor and still glean more grime. The floors needed scraping first, then sweeping, then scraping again and so on. How my arms ached! But at last all that could be removed by knife and broom was removed, and an enormous pile of filthy debris awaited destruction outside the front door. But before I could attend to that, before even I began on the windows or scrubbing the floor, there was something else that must be done. Those gaping rat-holes – I could not stand them any longer, they must be sealed.

So I went out to the ruins of the old barn and hunted about for likely pieces of wood. I felt very much like Robinson Crusoe searching the beach for useful oddments among the jetsam, or the more fortunate Swiss family visiting the wreck and making off with anything and everything useful. It was fun, this behaving like a shipwrecked mariner; it took away that gnawing hurt that tugged at my heart and numbed my mind – the effect of the chill isolation of the place. For even though it was a glorious day and I had been ceaselessly busy, the atmosphere of the cottage was constantly pressing upon me. I was conscious, too, of the rats. Although I had not seen a single one, I knew they were there; they were watching me, biding their time, I imagined. It made me uneasy. So like a boy out of detention, I found relief exploring the remains of the old farm buildings.

There was nothing standing except a few massive old oak posts and one low brick wall. I can't think how such complete destruction overwhelmed the buildings. There was no sign of fire; they just seem to have tumbled down, and then been looted by anyone who wanted a piece of timber for this, or some bricks for that. There were some fine pieces of old oak, a foot square, much assorted boarding, masses of broken slates, and all kinds of odds and ends, a veritable mine for a shipwrecked mariner. I collected a quantity of useful-looking board and returned to the cottage very much heartened.

It looked much better; in fact I was surprised how much I had done. How often that happens! You tackle a big job; you work hard, so hard you are scarcely aware of the results of your labours. At last you rest, or go off on some other task. When you resume, why, the task is done, or far more complete than you ever thought it was when you left it. So with Copsford, the whole place was actually swept from top to bottom. How different it looked! I was amazed.

With renewed energy I tackled the problem of the rat-holes in the best bedroom. I had remembered a hammer and nails before leaving the village, but I had no saw. Thus I could only select pieces of wood approximately the right length. But what did it matter, one board alone covered in seven holes. I made a merry din with the hammer, and it did the cottage good to hear. As I banged I wondered about the rats and what their reactions would be. Fifteen holes, fifteen holes, how many rats for fifteen holes? I fastened the wood grimly secure. Fifteen holes, fifteen rats? I had to use double thickness in places to cover the yawning cavities. Fifteen holes, fifty rats! Bang! bang! Yes, it was a declaration of war all right. Fifteen holes in one room, how many rats, how many rats? Bang! bang! It did Copsford good to hear, but the rats lay low, never a sign did they give – ah, but they were there.

Satisfied that at least one room was rat-proof, I felt more comfortable to get on with the cleaning of it. I washed the windows and the walls and the woodwork, and my single bucket of water was like mud. I slung it away and went and fetched more from a nearby pond. This was quite clean enough for preliminary washing. I had wasted my time carrying water from the farm. From then on I dipped all washing-water from the pond, the old farm-yard pond, I presumed, now ringed with rushes, reed mace and burreed, and only carried drinking water from the farmer's well.

I scrubbed the floor; and I'm afraid I used so much water on those old ill-fitting boards that a great deal of it went through and appeared in huge dull patches on the ceiling below. But the room became clean at last, and by dinner time I could lay my lunch on the floor, or the windowsill or the little narrow mantelpiece at will. I stopped work, and placing a board across two piles of bricks, I sat down to eat.

Copsford grew strangely silent. All the busy sounds of the morning, the cheerful hammering, my own voice I believe, had fled away. Like ooze creeping slowly back where footsteps have squelched it, flooding in, meeting, mixing, levelling, blotting out all trace, the chill quiet of the forgotten cottage returned. Charged with a numbing hopelessness, it drowned all trace of all I had done to infuse the place with the sound of human life and movement. It overwhelmed me. I just sat as if turned to stone, the unchewed crust in my mouth, the sandwich in my hand. I was dimly conscious of the cascading sunshine outside, and the soft purring of a pair of turtle doves somewhere in that seventh heaven; but between that and me was a great gulf fixed. A most intense depression weighed upon me, the hopelessness of it all; even if the place ever was clean how could I live between these hideous bare walls, faced with this sickly painted woodwork, carpeted with these rude, bare boards? How could I wash or drink, or cook,without a drop of dean water within a mile?

With the returning tide the rats came back. Not only had their sanctuary been violated but their very rights-of-way had been savagely blockaded. They too declared war. In the chill silence I was acutely aware of soft movements as they made their way unseen about the house, and as they came under the floor of the room, where I was sitting, to investigate the damage done to their highways. Now and again there was a tiny sound as a fragment of fallen plaster trembled at their touch. Once or twice a piece was dislodged and it fell between the lath-and-plaster walls with a tinkle magnified a thousandfold.

They were defeating me – the cottage and the rats; the slough of despond was closing over my head. It may seem absurd to those who read that I should have been so easily vanquished; but there are times that occasionally come when we are completely alone, cut off from all contact and intercourse with friends and acquaintances, when we are oppressed by the futility of all and every effort. It is more than procrastination; willpower is sapped, ambition withered, enthusiasm dead. No one is to blame but our own thinking, 'There is nothing good nor bad but thinking makes it so', but sometimes circumstances are so powerful that we yield to them and instantly a paralysis of inaction creeps upon us, both mental and physical.

I cannot quite tell how it happened, but while held prisoner in this Doubting Castle, an odd brick that I might have used for the support of the bench where I sat, overbalanced and fell flop on the floor. It startled me; the rats, taken altogether unforewarned, panicked. There was a wild rush, and just as on that first day when I visited the cottage, there was a terrifying cascade of sound. It effectively roused me from my trance. I sprang to my feet, and no doubt my hair stood on end. What was the cause? I don't know, I never did know. It seemed impossible that rats alone could do it, unless indeed there were scores of rats. But it was the second time that I had heard it, and I recovered quickly. Familiarity breeds contempt, and every time it occurred afterwards I grew more and more contemptuous. Unfortunately, just as I became really interested in it, and sought to discover exactly how it was caused, so did its intensity and volume decrease, until at last it ceased altogether.

I recovered. I swore total war on all rats. *Yes*, I would return forthwith to the village and buy poison – much poison. I would buy wallpaper and make paste, I would buy paint and brushes and stain, and I would beg, borrow or buy a dog.

The enemy

THE WAR

Rats people regard with very different feelings. There are some who think them no more unpleasant than mice or rabbits; almost invariably they describe them by the familiar adjective 'old', or call them all 'cunning old fellows'. Others there are who shudder at the very name, and the sight of one will send them into hysterics. My account of the rat war will please neither of these, for while I respected my enemies, I killed on sight, or in the most underhand way. It was to be the rats or I who should inhabit Copsford. There could be no place for both of us.

The village provided me with all I required except the dog, but the postman promised me something in that line, 'a nice little bitch, just the thing for rats'. The music mistress made me a bucket of paste. I borrowed brushes, bought rolls of wallpaper, a tin of paint, a tin of stain and two tins of rat poison. Thus equipped, I returned to give battle.

Who would have thought that the combatants would have come to grips so soon? The moment I entered the upper room where I had laboured all the morning, what should I see but a great rat surveying me from the far corner.

Hastily I closed the door and took stock of my antagonist. He also took stock of me. He crouched there with forepaws slightly raised and fixed me with horrid, unmoving, beady eyes. What to do? I could not politely open the door and invite him to make good his escape; that would have meant defeat. Yet I had no weapon whatever, except the tins of poison in my pocket, and a broken table-knife with which I had proposed to open the tins. It was fit for little else. Should I attack the rat with my bare hands, or attempt to stamp upon it with my London shoes?

Revolting thoughts – and at the same time all sorts of odds and ends of stories, real or exaggerated, fluttered through my mind about poisoned bites, and the fury and throat-leaping proclivities of cornered rats. I was uneasy, to say the least, and although since I have wondered why I did not slip out of the room and go and fetch a big stick or a handful of ammunition in the form of chunks of broken brick, such solutions never entered my mind. I was obsessed by the idea that the brute must be attacked there and then. There was no retreat, no time to call up reserves or artillery, the enemy must be dealt with immediately.

Bethought me of the poison, and keeping my eye continually on him, I slipped a tin from my pocket and removed the lid. He moved not a muscle, so, gingerly extracting a small helping, I zipped it in his direction. Slightly interested, the big rat moved an inch or two towards it, but it offended his nose, and he backed, and then ran a few feet beside the board which blocked his exits. I flipped more poison, which actually smoked upon the floor. He ignored it. Perhaps it annoys rats to be peppered with phosphorus, for at last he came to grips and began running fast along the skirting towards the door – and me.

Whether or not the rat was actually attacking me I cannot say, but in fewer seconds than it takes to read this line, I raised the knife-stump behind my shoulder and jerked it with vicious force at the oncoming rat. With an accuracy that I could not believe, and have never since equalled, the knife struck the rat behind the head, and in an instant the poor wretch was stretched on its back, kicking convulsively. Rushing forwards with a shout of triumph, I snatched up the knife and flung it three times at the thing as it lay twitching on the floor, and three times successively I missed, and the knife quivered in the floorboards.

It all sounds melodramatic now, but I could not stand the wretched creature lying there half dead, and those frantic throws of mine were only on account of an urgent desire to put it out of its misery. As it happened, I need not have worried, for the first blow must have broken its neck and killed it immediately.

I could bear it no longer and fled from the room, leaving the knife stuck fast in the floor less than an inch from my senseless foe.

Very sweet was the May sunshine. The undiscovered country, which had been calling me all the morning, now led me astray, and the magic of the marshland ensnared my feet and captured my imagination. Such country as I was exploring surpassed all dreams of childhood days. I wandered, never to meet a single soul, and yet beset by intense life, with not one common sound of human ways, and yet enriched with a hundred sounds of wings and wind, birdsong and running water. Small wonder I delayed. I caught the drifting scents of honeysuckle and sweet briar, mint and garlic; I dabbled in iron-rusted water, I watched the bleating snipe, I saw rare flowers and abundant herbs. I drank so deep of all these good gifts that Copsford and its rats dwindled to a molehill of impossibilities. But return to it I must.

Triumphantly I wrenched my knife-stump from the boards, for the rat was dead, stiff where he had fallen. But when I lifted the body by its naked tail I was shocked to see that fleas were already leaving the death-cold body of their host. With uneasy speed I cast the corpse forth, and returned with haste to trample out the life of this second threatening plague. I feared the last state of Copsford might be worse that the first and decided that the village must provide me with another kind of tin on the morrow.

First blood was to my credit, and the rats took the reverse seriously. They worried me no more that day. I sealed every hole that I could find, but not before I lost sight of a portion of poison down each. I banged and hammered and at last felt that it was impossible for any rat to run the blockade. The sun was near setting when I finished, and when I finally left, pulling the front door to behind me, and wedging a couple of bricks in the last hole, I was amused to think that I had no key.

The farmer had not found it yet. 'Where the mischief the danged thing had gone' he could not think. Neither did I care. I should have laughed at the idea of locking Copsford – to what purpose? Would tramps or vagabonds take a night's rest in such a lonely, rat-riddled, flea-infested cottage? Such folk rarely step far off the king's highway. In all my time at the cottage I never met one. There are no pickings in the unkempt countryside or in the tall quiet woods. And had there been any wandering soul with itching fingers, what could he have lifted in Copsford? I smiled. Even the borrowed buckets were not worth the toil across those rough pastures. Would locks and bolts keep out owls and bats when half a dozen broken panes invited them?

So I left the cottage, swept if not yet garnished, and as I looked back at it that quiet evening with the sunset all aglow behind it, it seemed that somehow it was changed. The windows were clean, and the soul of a house looks out of its eyes: sweet cottages peep, old houses blink and welcome. Now Copsford, which had at first defied, gazed after me at least as an acquaintance, and months later was even friendly. But I never knew a smile to wrinkle the hard corners of its eyes.

For a week I scrubbed, and cleaned, papered, whitewashed, painted and waged war. While at least one room became habitable, the war progressed ill. The rats would not again come to grips; instead they continued to persevere with their terror tactics. I persevered with traps and poison. I rolled tasty balls of cooked haddock and phosphorus; they vanished. I gave them a dish of it in the 'garden' at the back of the house. They made a banquet, and their friends at least must have come back for more. One tin of poison went nowhere; two, three, four and never a dead rat did I find. I set break-back mousetraps and caught mice till the tally got tangled up and I couldn't remember whether the score was forty-five or fifty-four. But enemy No. 1 lay low and published not their casualties. I brought to the front a small, almost toy rifle, which fired single bullets about the size of a dried pea. I kept it beside me as more accurate than a broken knife. Its moral support was considerable. It let me down, however, when I discovered that its spring was not equal to punching the pin into rim-fire cartridges with sufficient force to explode them. A Heath Robinson contrivance of elastic was therefore necessary. It had to be secured to the bolt and strained forward with the left hand halfway up the barrel. This was moderately efficient and three times out of five succeeded in firing the shot.

At last all was ready. In a milk float the farmer had conveyed my bedstead and bedding across the fields. The fences across the bridge had to be temporarily dismantled to allow for its passage, and when I saw the float and its cargo lumbering up the hill I was both elated and shocked. The Darn, my Rubicon, was crossed; the sanctuary of the hill was violated by a common cart and a still commoner iron bedstead. Already, you may observe, I had begun to live in a place apart. When we arrived at Copsford the farmer helped me to lift the chattels out and we leaned them up against the wall of the cottage. He very much wanted to look and see in what my week's work had resulted. But I could no more ask him in than I could have him or anyone else read this manuscript before it is finished. Some of us are like that; we cannot bear scrutiny, however kindly, of unfinished work.

'It do be strange to see them windows clean,' he said, looking curiously up at my bedroom window.

I agreed it must do after all those years.

'You'm really going to live here then?' he asked, scratching the back of his head and looking at me with screwed-up eyes.

'Why, of course,' I said, trying not to look too bewildered. 'I'm moving in tomorrow.'

He nodded his head solemnly. Then, suddenly mounting the float and shaking the reins like a charioteer, he shouted cheerfully above the din of its departure, 'I'll be fastening up the bridge agen.'

He was gone, and in a few minutes I heard the clang of the portcullis.

A few other journeys on foot sufficed to bring a chair, two small tables, a primus stove and elementary crockery to their respective places. All was ready; I had but to be shipwrecked.

I spent the last night in the village not without some misgivings. It had turned wet and windy, and as I sat in cosy kitchen comfort I could not help but picture that stark brick loneliness, draughty, rain-driven, far from human call, where on the morrow I would be. It was not to be dwelt upon.

The nice little bitch, promised by the postman, had not yet been delivered, and I was much disappointed. I'm afraid I must have shown this all too plainly, for the music mistress, always so thoughtful for my comfort, was insistent that I should borrow her dog. It was unthinkable that I should live out there without even a dog for company, she declared. This was kind, and I must say I was glad enough to accept. Fluff was a big collie.

He and I sat on the bed straining our ears. It was nearing midnight, and till now the rats had made no move. It was the first night in Copsford. The dog, after much sniffing and whimpering and scratching, had put himself down on the end of the bed, with his head a-stretch on his forepaws and eyes wide open, in that quaint way dogs have when pretending to rest. It was a fine, still night, and after we had come upstairs a deathly quiet had crept over the cottage. We muffled our breathing for fear we should be unable to hear. I had had no hesitation about undressing, but it is true I left things close to hand. I had put the candle out, and the moon, though not shining directly into the room, gave enough light to scare away imagination. For half an hour I had lain stiff, listening, listening, and not a sound stood out against that sinister, silent background. Then, almost as if I had passed into a fourth dimension, I suddenly became aware of movement all round me. There were whispers of movement above and below, in the walls and beyond the door. I was aware of the rat world, a world of darkness and twilight, of inky, tortuous tunnels that never see the light of day, of drainways and forgotten culverts, of 'tween-walls and cavities, of under-stacks and grime-smeared yards. I knew nose, whiskers, black-bead eyes thrust with infinite caution into the dusk, leaping shadows in the moonlight, and flying tails. All the odours of the rat world were in my nostrils; I knew the smell of sour ground and the musty underworld, the reek of foul drains and the stench of the muck-heap. I smelt rotting vegetation and mouldy grain, meal bags and stored potatoes. I knew the slash of cruel teeth and the taste of arm blood, the unwearying dig, dig, dig, the patient, persistent gnawing.

Cr-r-r-r-ump!

With a discomforting jerk I was back in my own world. The dog and I leapt on guard, hearts racing. A minute of suspense, and then another ugly crunch, followed by a tearing and splitting of wood, shattered our security. The rats were gnawing the blockade.

It was an unpleasant experience. How fast could rats gnaw? Judging by the determined repetition of that evil sound it would not be long before they were in the room. Cr-r-r-rump! How the sound tingled in my spine. I could feel the dog's back bristling as I held him back. He whimpered and strained against the collar. I had fantastic nightmares of the rats finding a weak spot in the blockade and pouring through in a torrent of revenge against me and all that I had done against them and their sanctuary – an undeserving Bishop Hatto. At last I thought they must be in the room and with a shout of rage I cast the dog loose, and simultaneously struck the wall to such good purpose with my fist that I felt the lath and plaster give and the newly hung wallpaper split.

Pandemonium broke loose. Yelping with excitement, Fluff ran round and round the room knocking over chair and table, and doing seemingly terrible execution. I, grasping the little gun and shouting encouragement, danced a fandango on the bed and strained the elastic so violently that the gun went off and a bullet ploughed through the bedclothes and buried itself in the floor. The rats, taken completely off their balance, went mad, making what sounded like a frenzied circuit of the blockade, and the roof, and the floor, a dozen times, before diving in ignominious rout to the ground below.

It was all terribly exciting. Never, surely, had Copsford witnessed such a bloody battle or smelled the reek of powder in her upper rooms. Scarce daring to put my naked foot to the floor, I groped about, trying to find candle and matches where they lay strewn upon the battlefield. At length the match spluttered, the broken wick caught and slowly grew into a flame that lit the wreck and 'shone round me o'er – the dead'?

Well, no, not quite. Wreckage there certainly was: book, candlestick, broken cup, my shirt and trousers, overturned chair and the rest – but dead, no, not one single mangled corpse could I discover. It was amazing. I looked at Fluff, half expecting him to have swallowed the lot. But he just grinned at me, with tongue lolling out and frothy saliva dripping on the floor. Somehow I felt the joke was on me and I sat on the bed and laughed, and he joined me, till we were exhausted. At length I tidied up the mess and took the candle on a tour of inspection. As was now to be expected, the blockade remained unrun, the outer perimeter of our defences had nowhere been pierced. Nevertheless it was a famous victory.

We courted sleep again, and although we heard occasional movements I have little more memory of that night. I am dimly conscious of an irritating gnawing which in my half-dreams seemed to be boring a hole in my head. But morning found me well rested, the dog licking my face, and the sun high.

With the night fairly won through, I felt that I was now really established in Copsford. I set the primus going and made my first cup of tea. How good that was! And bread, with butter from the farm, made a breakfast, which Fluff and I, sitting in the morning sun that streamed through the open door, thought second to none. But while the war is still in progress I must not digress on life and work in the cottage.

Truth to tell, after Blenheim I knew less and less of them. I think the poison was really getting to work and I continued to supply it unstintingly. However, a few days later I had two more sharp encounters which I must relate here.

The first – and most amazing – affair occurred one wet afternoon when my outdoor activities were brought to a standstill. I had come across some stronger than usual break-back mouse-traps during one of my excursions to the village shop, and what put it into my head that grey afternoon I cannot tell, but I thought that with one of these traps, properly baited and placed, I might be able to catch a rat. But rats are strong and determined beasts, and I knew only too well that if I did catch a rat by head, leg or tail, it could just as easily make away with my trap secured to its person as carry off a potato. Rats, too, have a terrible, crude courage, and in their frenzied desire to escape from a trap will not stop at self-mutilation, or amputation, to secure their freedom. I have, on more than one occasion since, seen the torn skin and a severed limb left in the jaws of those cruel clam traps. I often wonder what happens to these wretched legless creatures; no doubt they soon die, or are destroyed by their own kind. It seems to be the rule of the wild to exterminate those of their kind which are deformed, wounded or unnatural. No doubt it is because they appear to behave strangely and hence are regarded as hostile. But to my trap, which, to prevent its being carried away, I secured by a long wire through the open scullery window to a brick indoors. It was baited with a piece of tough cheese rind, set rather stiffly and placed in a run which I had detected in a tangle of vegetation behind the outhouse.

I retired to my upstairs room, leaving open the door so as to be sure to hear the jangle of the wire should I have a catch.

It was a miserable afternoon. Rain drove across the countryside, not in straight lines but in ragged wisps and shaggy grey curtains. It was the kind of day that eats the heart out of a lonely man. One sits and stares. There are lots of things indoors with which one might usefully occupy oneself, but the gloomy devil says, 'What's the good, what's the good on a day like this?' Sanity replies, 'You must do something. If you're not going to get on with writing, which you came here to do, why not get on with the painting of the woodwork?' 'No good,' says the devil, 'of course you can't write brightly on a day like this; and as for painting, don't be absurd, the woodwork is streaming with damp; no good at all.' Sanity answers weakly, 'For goodness' sake do something; you'll go potty sitting here staring out of the window doing nothing.' The gloomy devil answers, 'No good doing anything this afternoon; look at the time, not worth starting anything now.' I stare out of the uncurtained window, whose streaming panes contort the already distorted landscape, and listen to these nagging voices, hearing and seeing nothing else. Time and again I dip my pen in the ink, and time and again the ink dries on the nib and never a word do I write. The rain is so heavy that it clouds across the valley of the Darn and shuts out all the saddened landscape beyond the hill, and I am as alone and cut off as a mountaineer cloud-bound upon a desolate peak.

Not quite alone: my eye suddenly catches a movement among the drenched tussocks below me and to my surprise it is a large black cat. which in spite of its bulk is picking its dainty way through the rain-bowed herbage towards the ruin of the barn. Like the sequence of events which followed upon the old woman going to market and buying a pig, so that cat reminded me of mice, mice of rats, rats of my rats, my rats of my trap. Good, something to do, and though it seemed ridiculous so soon to expect results, I cautiously descended the stairs and peered out through the scullery window. The wire had certainly been moved, and I found it quite impossible to follow the line of it through that tangle of vegetation; neither could I see the trap. I felt like a fisherman who has dozed and then suddenly roused to feel his line tugging but his boat nowhere. I ran, not for my landing-net but for the little gun, and laying it handy by, seized the wire and dragged the trap from among the rank weeds. It came like an evil fish, pulling and jerking. Ugh! What a gruesome catch was mine! In the trap was a rat's head, no more.

One can only put two and two together and make five. But consider: the rat easily caught by its head and the spring of the trap too weak to break that strong neck, the creature leaping and writhing at the end of the wire, the advent of the black, fierce, half-wild cat, which watches the slowly wearying antics of its prey; the cat then seizes its opportunity and makes the meal of its life but cannot detach the head; it stealthily makes away, very full, to its lair amongst the ruins of the barn, and only the gnawed head with its horrid, beady eyes remains to tell the tale. Is not the sum complete?

I was much heartened by this success. The gloom of the afternoon was forgotten. The trap was re-set. I took tea like a lord in the upper room, and then, donning wellingtons and mackintosh, I trudged my squelching way to the village to be still further encouraged by more good news. The postman had left word in the office that the little bitch was waiting for me whenever I cared to call at his house. Right glad I was to hear this, for Fluff I had to return to his mistress, and it had been grim without his company. So forthwith I called on the postman.

Floss, he said, was a Shetland collie, and I did not know whether to take him seriously or not, for I must admit I had never heard of such a breed. I said she reminded me of a Manx Sheepdog. It was tit for tat, for he looked at me quite seriously and said he wished he could get hold of such a dog. I nearly said by the tail, and we could have had a good laugh; but we were both conscious of our ignorance. Seven-and-six solemnly changed hands, and he gave into my keeping the piece of string which served as both lead and collar. Floss was mine.

It is scarcely fair to Floss to give this account of her sale before introducing her. She was all the postman said, except perhaps the breed, and much more than a 'nice little bitch'. She had the build of a small collie but the head and manner was that of a lakeland sheepdog. She had no tail. There was just the suggestion of a stump which, when she was pleased, set a little tassel oscillating, but to look at she was as bereft as a Manx cat. Her hair was as silky as a cocker and as black. There were one or two small patches of tan, two exquisite brown dimples above the eyes, and a slender white front. The eyes were the soft brown eyes of a dog that serves one master only. This I learnt in course of time, and when I knew, I always wondered how it was that Floss transferred so easily, so sweetly, so graciously, from, to whomsoever she belonged, through the postman, to me. But dogs have a sixth sense, have they not? They know not only what is afoot but also what is to be. Floss trotted patiently beside me that wet evening, across the drowned fields and over the Darn, and never once did she drag or pull or whimper to go back. Across the bridge, I slipped the rough strong collar over her head and, delighted, she ran loose, circling in that mad, gay way that dogs have, and coming back to me with merry eyes and lively, wind-blown ears. She was mine already, and she was first at Copsford, waiting for me on the step.

Next day I had my last encounter with the rats and Floss won her spurs.

It was shortly after breakfast that I was suddenly startled by a bout of sharp, fierce barking. It was Floss's first warning, and it took me by surprise. The noise came from the outhouse and the bark was so imperative that I snatched up the little gun and hastened to her assistance.

The floor of the outhouse was littered with the decaying rubbish of many years' forgetfulness. Now and again, I suppose, the farmer had put odd sacks of this and that for shelter and storage in the outhouse, following the line of least resistance, because he never could lay hands on the danged key, and take the trouble to put the leftovers in the safe keeping of the cottage. When he did remember what he had left, by the time he went to fetch it no doubt weather and rats had long since played havoc with it. Anyway there was the floor of the outhouse choked with half-filled sacks spilling their mouldy contents through ragged holes which generations of rats had spent their leisure hours in tearing.

Amid this promising cover Floss had found her game, and there she was, yapping and bridling with excitement and importance. Gingerly I moved a sack or two with the muzzle of the little gun. Floss buried her nose behind them and drew in great snuffs and then blew the dust out again in fierce snorts. No rat was forthcoming. I grew bolder and moved more rubbish from the wall… nothing. Floss grew frantic with excitement, darting first to where I laboured and then back to the opposite wall, and there she began scratching with furious determination, sending out spurting showers of rotting clover from between her hind legs. Ah! There it is. It is running round the wall I have just cleared, towards the door. 'Floss, Floss!' Oh, so slow, she does not see it amid the fury of her digging. It will escape. I follow it with the muzzle of the little gun. It is six inches from the door. The elastic cuts my hand, bang! The spurt of fire seems to envelop the rat. 'Floss, Floss, here dog, here!' She sees it struggling and snaps like lightning, backs as though it were a dangerous serpent, in again and a frightful shake. Crack, and it falls limp on the stone floor.

'Good dog, good Floss, rats!'

She picks it up and, with her head held high, trots away, the trailing naked tail threatening a stumble in her pride.

And that was the last rat I saw alive in and about Copsford. Floss, I think, must have taken a heavy toll, for she was the most persevering ratter I have ever known. But she kept her kills to herself, never parading them before me. She took them away, as she did that first one, and hid them or buried them, patting the soil down firm and smooth with her muzzle. The noises in the house gradually died away, the well-defined runways about the cottage overgrew and disappeared. The enemy was wiped out to the last rat. The war was won.

TO WORK

THE TASK OF CLEANING the cottage and making but one room habitable had taken longer than I had expected. The days were slipping by, and if I, single-handed, had attempted to do to the other four rooms what I had accomplished in the bedroom, the days would have been weeks.

The bedroom was cleaned, papered, whitewashed. The floor was stained, the woodwork painted. The windows were uncurtained, and there was nothing on the floor. I had a bed, a table and chair. It was primitive, but here I could retire at least to decency and clean comfort. But in the other rooms, beyond the most vigorous cleaning I did not go. There really was no need. In the large downstairs room I set up, as a table, a big door from the ruins of the barn. On it I had my primus, my odd crockery and a tin or two for food. On it I cooked, and served most of my meals; only on important occasions did I serve them to the gentleman in the bedroom. There were two cupboards in the large room, and a sort of cupboard-larder in the corner which ran back under the stairs. As there was no ventilation in any of these, the air was always so musty I could never think of keeping food in them.

Fantastic growths of woolly mould, both blue and green, quickly covered the first food I left on those shelves. Not only that, but legions of queer beasts haunted those recesses and came and preyed upon my leavings. No amount of scrubbing could reach them in their strongholds. Stuff which should kill bugs, fleas, moths and beetles could not cope with them. Perhaps because I did not use enough, often enough. So I gave it up and was quite content keeping all food in bug-tight tins on the table.

I was not going to allow cooking to worry me. I could boil and fry on the primus, but cooking and baking were quite beyond me. It would have been a waste of time and labour for me to bring ingredients from the village and prepare myself puddings and joints and cakes, when I could easily buy prepared foods which would keep indefinitely in tins and cartons and be no worry to me at all in preparation. I had no one to please but myself, and if some days I lived entirely on bread and farm butter, and cups of tea, nobody grumbled, and the washing-up used none of my precious water. I kept the water in a large billycan under the table.

Otherwise the big room was quite bare. The great hole round the hearth I filled with rubble and tidied up with bricks. It was then level enough and safe enough for a fire. In the wreck of the barn I found two pieces of bent and jointed iron which made excellent firedogs. The scullery was too cold and bare to be of any use except when I was specially pressed for space. I often wondered what the good housewife of thirty years agone must have said about it. Of all the badly planned corners of a cottage that was one. Everyone going up and downstairs had to pass through it. Imagine the wet, the mud, the steam, the angry language that went up the stairs. Imagine a main family thoroughfare through your scullery. Only Floss had that right through mine. The two rooms upstairs were thoroughly clean and rat-proof, and that was all I needed to be able to start upon my work. So I must now disclose what the proposed work was that had brought me to Copsford. In London, up in that third-floor-back, I had just managed to keep myself on the uncertain income of a freelance journalist. Although it is heartbreaking work collecting rejection slips, I had been prepared for it, and no doubt had more successes than I deserved. But I was not one of those brass-fronted fellows who interview the refuse collectors at their work and write up in popular journalese what happens to millions of tons of this and that that passes under their muck-rakes. I tried, but deservedly

failed; my heart was not in it. I was of the country. I could not dip my pen in the lifeblood of the city streets. I needed the very song of the shadow-dappled brook to write, with the sound of wild wings in my ears and the scent of wildflowers in my nostrils.

In the country, however, one is miles from editors' offices; post delays; competition with well-established contributors is severe. In the country the unknown writer does not live by words alone, he must turn his hands to other tasks. During my chequered freelance career it had been my fortune – fate if you will – to come into contact with someone who knew all about the collecting and harvesting of wild herbs. The work appealed to me tremendously, and though at the time it never for a moment entered my head that it was work that I myself might do, yet the seed was sown and in time I found myself dallying with the idea. Soon I was going into the matter more thoroughly than ever I would have done for a magazine article. I had interviews, I read books and pamphlets. I was even brass-fronted enough to call on a famous firm in the East End and have a chat with the buyer. I am grateful to him that he never snubbed or sneered. I learnt much and was convinced on two points.

First, that certain wild herbs of the English countryside, if properly collected and properly dried, could be sold if offered in the right places. Second, that if one gave one's whole time to it during the season, financially it would scarcely yield enough to keep one the year round. There were alternatives. If one could buy land and cultivate certain rare, high-priced herbs, there might be more in it. Or if one organised a centre to which many small quantities might be brought by children, or idlers or holidaymakers or other cheap labourers, then a sufficiently large quantity might be amassed to pay the organiser. It was plain that neither of these courses suited me. I had no capital and could not begin to think of waiting for a year or two until I could sell my first harvest. As to organising a centre, while I was willing certainly to accept herbs which anyone was industrious enough to collect for me, to spend my time organising cheap labour and nothing else, to send out hordes of careless collectors, rambling and scrambling all over the precious countryside, I never could and never would do it. Furthermore, Copsford Herb Centre would be more than a mile from the road and near two miles to the station. Who was going to collect and carry all the odd quantities those distances?

I knew I must do the harvesting alone. I alone must do the collecting and supervise the drying, and handle the packing. It was to be a one-man show. I must give my whole time to it during the season. Only when the weather made collecting impracticable would I write, and in the winter months then would I catch up on the literary work. Thus would I make ends meet. Thus would I escape the city and live as I had often imagined and desired, right against the heart of nature.

CLIVERS

ALL WAS READY. Copsford stood swept, awaiting garnishing. Spring smiled through the broken window, beckoned through the open door. I heard her voice. I smelled the perfume of her garments. Her touch was upon my forehead. I must up and out and away. I was a Green Man. I must hie to the lanes and the hedgerows, to tangled banks and woodland jungles, there to search and gather clivers.

Clivers, cleavers, goosegrass, sweetheart, it is all one. Quaint, square-stemmed, trailing green stuff, so decked with countless tiny hooks that it seems to stick wherever it touches. Tenaciously does it cling to my shirt, my shorts, my socks. It winds about my bare legs and arms till they tingle and smart. I am studded inside and out with a hundred rounded seeds. I carry them with me in my hair and my bosom. I gather, gather, gather. I pull it from the hedges that line the winding lanes. I scramble it down from rough, weedy banks. I unravel it from among brambles and stinging nettles. I weed it from the hedges of the cottagers and many a curious glance I get, and words sometimes.

'What are you doing, my man?'

'Weeding your hedge of this green stuff, marm.'

'You ain't doin' that for nothing, I know.'

'Yes, marm, I am, and I'll take it all away if you've no objection.'

Occasionally they mumble something about being up to no good, but usually, kind souls, they have no objection, and one charming dame was effusively grateful to the Quixotic man who cleared from her front-garden hedge that tangle of cleavers that strangled it. She was inquisitive, too, of course; what did I do with it? What did I want it for? But that it was a herb which I was harvesting was all I could tell her. I did not know for certain how the herbalists might use it, though its tonic properties are quite well known.

Clivers is common everywhere, especially along the edges of old cultivated or disturbed ground. That is to say, it is common because one so frequently sees it on a country walk. But if you start gathering it to amass a quantity, then you discover that while it is common, it is certainly not abundant. You can walk many dusty miles along lanes and ditches and the total bag may be much less than twenty pounds in weight. And the longer you carry it the lighter it grows. It loses moisture very rapidly; wind and sun dry it as you walk along, or where you leave it in bundles ready to be collected when you return. Many a bulky bundle that I could scarcely wield, thirty pounds or more in weight when freshly picked, has been twenty-five by the time I brought it to the scales in Copsford. However hard I worked, the result was always disappointing on the scales. Often I thought the old postal spring balance that I bought for the job must be out of its reckoning. But no, it told the truth, and it is still in order today. There is a fascination about herb-gathering which I felt from the very first day. It is not merely the satisfaction of having gathered something good and useful from wild and waste and unwanted places, not merely the atavistic urge to harvest, not only the close contact with nature, but something of all three, mingled with the delights of liberty.

One afternoon in early June, the music mistress, who was much interested in my herb-harvesting, came with me in search of clivers. We took bicycles so that we might go far afield; and down the winding lanes, up forgotten byways, we walked and trundled many a mile. She too felt the urge to gather, more and yet more sweetheart. We made great bundles, we festooned our bicycles with it, from head to foot we were covered with the little double-round seeds. It was all great fun, we experienced the lighthearted joy of children. We were sorry when at last it was time to return our bicycles and to dump our huge bundles on the other side of the farmer's lane-side gate. The music mistress said she had enjoyed the gathering very much; and so had I, and I hoped she would come again.

'Perhaps,' I ventured, 'one day you will come over to Copsford to see it all drying.'

'Perhaps I will,' she said.

The return journey across the fields seemed lonelier than usual. I had to leave one of the bundles at the farm so that I might have one hand free to carry milk and water; and right glad I was after toiling to the top of the hill to see Floss waiting for me. Dear dog, how patiently she waited, setting her guard over the cottage. Almost always I had to leave her there when out gathering, not because the cottage really wanted any guarding, but because the farmers and gamekeepers, across whose lands and preserves I wandered, were never pleased to see a dog at large. However well trained, however much under control, they never credited a dog with being harmless. I do not blame them; I too have seen and heard far too much of stray dogs hunting at large. Not that I blame the dogs themselves. What more natural than that a dog should chase a rabbit that springs up under his nose! What more inevitable than that pheasants and partridges should be disturbed from their dust-baths by a racing, yelping dog, nose to ground, searching for more rabbits! The average farmer doesn't care the snap of his fingers about a dog chasing rabbits, and as for the game birds, they can well look themselves. But it is these untrained, usually inexperienced town dogs that do serious damage. They chase chicken and ducks, which, quite unable to look after themselves, are slaughtered. They chase and worry sheep, maiming and even killing lambs and ewes.

So Floss was left behind when I went gathering. What she did all those long hours I often wondered.

Yet she was always at her post. No matter what hour I returned, there she was, lying on the doorstep if she had not heard my coming; or if she had, she was standing at the tumble-down fence, all a-tremble with delight, her soft ears often pricking in the breeze. And she would never leave her post until I whistled. Then like a stone from a sling she raced towards me, and round and down, and then she would lie on her back quite still, and await either a rub of her chest or a sharp 'Up!' Then round and round she would race in delirious circles as if the very devil were after her tail tassel. And she would yelp as if he pulled it, and turn such tight corners that her shoulders seemed to brush the ground. Ah, she was a good companion for a lonely man.

Sedately she walked back with me to the farm to fetch the other bundle of clivers, and it was dusk by the time we had them on the scales. They were 28 lb and 22 lb. I had almost expected 30 and 40 lb, but still I was not too disappointed. Fifty pounds of clivers in one afternoon was a good harvest, and I never equalled it. But the work was not ended by bringing the bundles to Copsford. It all had to be shaken apart and hung up to dry, and that took me until the moon filled the uncurtained windows. Copsford was garnished. At first I had thought that most of my herbs would have been dried by laying them out on shelves made of garden netting. In the darker upstairs room I had erected a rough framework from floor to ceiling, in which were stretched, on either side of a narrow gangway, tier on tier of shelf netting. It looked imposing and most businesslike, but when it came to laying out 50 lb of fresh herb it was hopelessly inadequate, and for stuff like clivers, most unsuitable. This tangle of clinging trailers is difficult enough to separate, but to attempt to spread it out on string net is a hopeless proposition. So I had to fall back on improvisation, and soon found the simplest method of drying it was to hang it over lines of string like so much untidy washing.

Along two opposite walls of the big downstairs room, about a foot from the ceiling, I hammered in a series of nails about eighteen inches apart. Between these my clothes-lines were tightly stretched, and thus it was the simplest matter possible to detach a hank of clivers, pull it apart and toss it over the line. There it hung in lanes, readily accessible, perfectly aired, easily turned over, and when dry lifted off without tangle or loss. It was a satisfactory scheme, but I have not heard of anyone else repeating it.

The drying of herbs is a most important part of the business, and one can only learn it by experience. It is no good trying to hurry the operation; to attempt to hasten it by sun-drying or artificial heating almost always means loss of quality and a poor colour. Clivers dried in the sun goes brown and shrivelled and brittle; whereas slow, even drying leaves it a good glossy green colour, pliable, without moisture, yet still rich in its essential properties. If taken from the drying-room too soon, and this is very easy to do in hot, dry weather, and stored away in sacks, one has the horrible experience a few weeks later, when opening the mouth of the sack to inspect the contents, to discover a fine, white, dusty mould developing all over it. It may mean a whole sackful ruined, perhaps the equivalent of 200 lb of fresh herb. Clivers dries very light, about 5 to 6 lb of fresh herb shrinking down to 1 lb of dry.

If the herb is taken too late from the drying-room, and this quite frequently happens when a spell of dry weather suddenly succeeds a long, damp, slow-drying period, the plant is so brittle that it crumbles to dust. The rosette of pale-green leaves of cleavers is so slight that there is always some loss with this herb at the bagging-up time, but that is better than mould. Other herbs, if allowed to become too dry, just cannot be handled; they smash and crumble and fall away into useless fragments. Others again – a few – one never seems to be able to dry enough; they always feel moist or oily to the touch, no matter how many days they hang on the line.

Perhaps I shall weary you with the technicalities of herb-drying, but it was absorbingly interesting to me, for I was charged with enthusiasm, when once I got started, to gather and harvest herbs of first-class quality. When it came to the time to sell, I wanted to offer stuff second to none, and spared no pains to be able to do so. My herbs were to be of good colour, excellent content, and pure. The first was achieved by proper drying and by gathering when weather conditions were good, the second by gathering when the plants were at their best and with careful drying and storing, the last by not allowing one stem or leaf of any other plant to become entangled and mixed with it. I must say the last caused me the most trouble, especially with clivers, for these long trailing stems, armed with their thousands of tiny hooks, seized hold of a hundred odds and ends, leaves, twigs, stems, grasses and the like. Time did not usually allow for these to be removed until the herb was hanging on the lines in the drying-rooms, where I spent many hours walking up and down the lanes sorting it out, the changes in colour during the drying sometimes making it easy, sometimes making it increasingly difficult, to detect.

I had many problems to solve, many difficulties with which to contend, but it was that over which I had no control – the weather – that dominated everything that happened at Copsford, and determined day by day, often hour by hour, what I should or should not do. A few hours' rain in the morning brought all gathering to a standstill for that day. Herbs must not be collected wet on any account. Heavy dews would delay gathering until afternoon. Dried herb was like a sponge ready to absorb moisture at the first opportunity. In damp weather I had to keep a small oil stove going day and night in the storage room, and this meant paraffin as well as drinking water and milk to be brought daily from the lane-side. Spells of warm, dry weather were intensively busy. Everything to be done at once and only one pair of hands to do it. Herb to be removed from the strings and shelves, herb to be bagged up, herb to be gathered, herb to be laid out and hung up to dry, more and yet more herb to be collected.

The weather ruled all, and I often thought of all those millions in London, and indeed in every town and city, to whom changes in the weather meant no more than carrying or not carrying a gamp to the station, office or workshop; all those for whom work went on just as ever it had done, no matter whether skies were blue or grey, no matter whether the sparkling dew drenched the awakening countryside, no matter whether the wind set hard and dry in the east or wet and billowy from the west. And I wondered, wondered at the artificiality of their lives, cut off from natural loveliness, variety and life, and I found increasing zest and joy in mine. True, spells of wet weather drove me to the gentleman's bedsitting room where I would mope, depressed by the unending procession of lowering rain clouds, and the ceaseless shudder of the old windows, but the busier I became the happier I was, and all the summer lay before me.

Clivers was my first harvest and perhaps this was one reason why it was so dear to me. I discovered a place where it grew in riotous profusion. There was a meander of the Darn enclosing a tongue of lowland over which, after a heavy rainfall, the brook invariably flooded, spilling rich mud in all directions. It was crowded with tall, lichen-hung alders, and ash, hazel and hawthorn, and one or two water-logged oaks. It was remarkable in having a number of lagoon-like pools and deep mud-filled gullies, all rust-red with iron, treacherously lidded with scum and bog plants, startlingly dangerous to unwary walkers. Here in early spring dog's mercury provided an unbroken carpet with dark-green pile, knee-high; later, all along the banks of the brook wild garlic massed its pale broad leaves and starry flowers, looking for all the world like lily-of-the-valley. Kingcups fringed the lagoons, and rank, square-stemmed figwort opened its dusky mouths five and six feet high above the water. There were burdocks with enormous rhubarb leaves and crimson-crowned, round-headed flowers, which clawed at you with their hooked scales. There were spearwort and thistles and nettles and when I found it, in it and through it and over it all there was clivers.

Sheaves of it thrust up around the alder trunks, matted rugs overlaid the mercury carpet, festoons and tapestries hung from fallen boughs, curtains screened the pools; such tangles tied together the brambles and nettles and thistles that impenetrable jungles were created.

Clivers has tiny white-star flowers, quite inconspicuous, but its innumerable square interlacing stems, set with numberless rosettes of narrow leaflets, make pattern and design complex beyond our imaginations' devising. Cleavers, goosegrass, sweetheart, ah, you have found a way to entwine and entangle my heart! We are all interwoven in such a pattern. Never do I see your up-rushing stems in spring but I remember those days when I carried you in great bundles for the garnishing of Copsford. Never do I forget one afternoon when I pulled your trailers from the country hedgerows and plucked your thousand clinging seeds from the hair and garments of my companion.

FOXGLOVE AND CENTAURY

NEAR THE RUINS OF BARN AND BYRE, right on the top of the hill was a small pond. In days of yore it must have been the farmyard pond, muddied with the paddling hoofs of the herd as they came and stretched their necks to drink, the scene of many a brood of domestic ducklings making arrowy speed from their distracted foster mother. Now it was a wild place, thickly fringed with reed mace and rushes, with water grasses trailing their long spears across its surface. There were no fish, but newts and frogs abounded, and a pair of waterhens had nested. Pond skaters dimpled the surface and cut fairy patterns as they glided magically across the mirrored sky, and slender metallic dragonflies poised on over-arching reeds or flitted to and fro above the skaters.

It was a charming little pool, as wild almost as a tarn on the moors, yet it lay barely twenty yards from Copsford. On several mornings during my first two weeks at the cottage I went out to look at it, alight in the early sunshine, and I wished I had the courage to plunge in. That I did not do so at once can be attributed to two reasons: one, that the pool was right on top of the hill in full view of the farm, a mile away; two, that I was born in the last year of the reign of Queen Victoria. This casts no mud at that illustrious queen; it simply means that in my childhood the little boy did not go without his top, even at the seaside, except in the greatest secrecy or in an atmosphere of extreme naughtiness. How absurd those days were. Nevertheless, the slave-collar of convention left an indelible scar. Although there was now no collar, I was acutely conscious of having worn it and of still feeling its restraint. To strip in the open air and plunge into unconventional water, even though the nearest sightseer was a mile away, was next to impossible for me. But giant circumstance proved too strong even for convention. The water I needed for drinking and cooking was a simple matter to transport by billycan from the well at the farm, it was a routine daily task. Water for washing, however, was another matter; a pailful went nowhere, but a pailful was an awkward load across rough and often slippery ground. Water from the Darn was quite clean and I had already carried some to the cottage for bathing. But if I brought water from the brook to bathe in at the cottage, why on earth did I not bathe in the brook? It seemed obvious enough, and if I were to bathe in the brook, why not in this little pond, barely twenty yards from my front door, my own private bathing pool?

At last came a morning in June, light, airy and still. I had awakened to find the early sun streaming in my open uncurtained window, golden and warm. I tossed away the bedclothes to stand entranced at the sight and sound and perfume of the perfect morning. It sometimes happens, at rare moments in our lives, we are suddenly aware of an altogether new world, different completely from that in which we commonly live. We feel as though we stand at the threshold of an undiscovered kingdom; for brief moments we understand life interpreted, we perceive meaning instead of things. In those golden minutes I understood every word on a single page of the magic book of Life inscribed in a language neither written nor spoken. There was a sublime tranquillity in the level white mists of the valley, a symphony like the ascending melodies of Grieg in the sun rays that climbed aslant the hill, a quiet strength in the stillness of the trees, a brotherhood of life in all living things. I was no longer a single life pushing a difficult way amidst material things, I was a part of all creation.

Strange sentiments these for a mere Green Man, and it will appear something of an anti-climax that my immediate reaction to those moments of exultation was to slip from the cottage with only a towel and plunge into the sunlit pool.

It was a baptism into a saner way of living and thinking. The soreness of the slave-collar was salved. It was an outward and visible sign on my inward awareness of at-one-ment.

True, I felt as though all the world were watching. The folk at the farm, I felt, must be lined up purposely to see what I was about; every bush and tree must be hiding someone who had come out that very morning to find out what went on at Copsford. But as I lay afloat between mud and sky, I realised suddenly, and with amusement, that only the lark on the wing could see me in the pool, the rushes and reed were a complete screen from all else.

Wild, unconventional water had always held a fascination for me, and from that day onwards was irresistible. In pool and brook, in lake and mountain torrent, in high tarn on moor and fell, I have found joy and inspiration. It is not just the tonic effect of water on the body that refreshes one; delightful as that may be, it is insignificant by comparison with the effect upon the mind. One escapes the chains of old ideas, one sheds threadbare thoughts, the grime and dirt and sweat of the commonplace are cleansed away. One's mind floats, no longer sunken under the dead weight of ordinary futilities, but buoyed up, it is carried along on new currents and catches heavenly reflections.

I am not alone in my joy in strange waters; many others must feel the same fascination. It is hard to find a reason. My mother was a fine and buoyant swimmer. In spite of all the impedimenta of Victorian bathing costumes, she loved the sea. No one rode the waves so lightly as she, and consequently we children were encouraged, though never driven, to do likewise.

Although I soon learned to swim, I never inherited my mother's skilful grace; but in spite of my clumsy style and the unpleasant effects of water in my ears, I too loved the sea. The irksome conventions of the beach were like iron, hard-cast and unquestioned, and I remember the loose, ugly, entangling bathing 'costume' with distaste. Besides, I was not one who found pleasure in beach crowds; much of the majesty, serenity and secrecy of the sea are lost in boisterous, paddling, splashing company.

Yet perhaps because part of my childhood was spent in sound of the sea, perhaps because my mother quietly showed what a wonderful thing water is, perhaps, as the dubious might say, on account of some mental kink, the thrill of adventuring in strange water was born and bred within me. Now after long years of unconscious repression I rediscovered it – in the old farmyard pond, gone wild, on the top of the hill.

To get out of the pond I floundered in much mud which squelched through my toes and buried my ankles. It does not sound very pleasant, but somehow it did not worry me very much. Sitting on a rush tussock, I rinsed it all away and felt ready to run and dance in that early morning June sunshine. This, I am afraid, would have attracted the attention of the farm folk in earnest, so I slipped into the wilderness and privacy of the cottage garden, there to dry and maybe to leap and dance too, and to feel the warm sun on my bare body. It was a memorable morning.

Many a morning after that, and, in fact, at all times of the day, the pool and I embraced one another. I got over the mud problem by dragging a sheet of corrugated iron from the ruins and sinking it just at the margin where I slipped in and out. It vanished from sight, but I knew exactly where it lay, and could be certain every time that my feet would land on it when I jumped in. It kept my feet clean and towels too. Thus the water problem, among far more important things, was solved at Copsford. Nor was I content with the pool, but soon went adventuring in the deep reaches of the brook, and found densely screened glades into which the summer sun streamed, where by slow degrees the sad pallor of my skin was changed to new bronze.

All these adventures are associated with foxglove and centaury, for this was the herb harvest which followed clivers. From foxglove is prepared the medicine digitalis, frequently used for its effect upon the heart. The search for it sent me far and wide through deep woods and forest rides, into flowery clearings and bracken-clothed commons. I was no longer a fellow of the open lanes and hedgerows, I became a denizen of the woods. I travelled by spinney and copse, through shaw and forgotten corduroy, at first because there I expected to find my herbs, but later because I became secretive and shy. Living so close to the wild, almost instinctively I copied creatures of the wild. I travelled swiftly, silently and unseen. I learned woodland behaviour, I heard woodland sounds.

Foxglove follows the woodcutter. Where woods are tall and deep and dark there is no undergrowth. Seeds lie dormant, bulbs and roots feebly sprout in early spring, but before ever they have a chance to grow or blossom, darkness shuts them in and they turn yellow and wither away and wait. Sometimes they wait, ten, twenty, thirty years; so much depends upon the whim of the landowner, or the energy of the farmer, or the fickle demands of industry, or the cruel curse of war. But inevitably the time comes when the knock-knock of the long-handled axe sounds through those quiet aisles.

A grievous scene of destruction follows. The long poles of hornbeam and ash, birch and alder are tumbled hither and thither in what seems hopeless confusion. Bleeding stumps are surrounded by countless staring chips, enormous tangled heaps of unwanted brushwood accumulate. The swish and drag of the great crosscut saws is added to the clatter of the axes. The nervous cry of yawing wood, the shout of the lumberjacks, the shivering sigh of falling timber, the startling crash and thunder of stricken giants, these are the sounds of the doomed woodland.

Then come the lorries and the waggons, the horses and tractors, and the long steel cables of the haulers, and the prostrate, limbless giants are dragged unceremoniously away. Mud and mire and sawdust, and smashed branches, and the ashes of great fires are left behind. Sometimes the wreckage is tidied up, the brushwood burnt, the cordwood sawn and carted away. But more often than not this is too expensive, or too much trouble, and the tangled, tumbled confusion, is left untouched. There are few sadder sights than this desolation, which so short a time before was the many-pillared temple of Pan, lulled by the sleepy croon of ring doves.

The following spring performs the miracle. Light, be it sunlight, moonlight, cosmic rays or all three, pierces the soil, awakens the sleepers, bestirs the languid, heals the wounded, and behold, leaf and blossom spring from darkness into light. Primroses come peeping where we never dreamed they had been; dog violets spread a purple carpet over sore places; lavishly are scattered the golden stars of celandines; windflowers, like a milky way, reach to distances. We stand dumbfounded before the magic of bluebells as they change to violet and hyacinth and ultramarine when sunshine and cloud shadow glide across them. Buds burst unexpectedly from the ill-treated stumps, tender shoots of ash and birch spring upward. A wonderful new woodland beset with blossom has come to life.

All the first year other biennials are developing root and stock, and in the second spring and summer there is a profusion of flowers beyond our wildest dreams. This is when foxglove astonishes us with its multitude of spires and bells. As a child I was amazed that it should be a wildflower. 'Who planted them all?' I asked in ecstatic wonder; and from the height of a little child one looks right into the purple-spotted mouths and sees the bees busy within and is overawed by those tapering spires high above one's head. What a world was that in which to live! What a world to recapture! Where the ground was churned by wheels and feet and hauled trunks springs centaury. I grew very fond of this slender little herb with its gay pink clusters of blossom. It is such a child of the light that its flowers will only open in the sunshine. In my diligent search for it, it led me into many a garden of Eden, little clearings where recently had stood a forest giant but which now was a flowery oval, hedged densely about by the two-or-three-year green of sweet chestnut and young birch and hazel. Often foxglove stood sentinel about the place, and later ragwort and rosebay and St John's wort. And when I pushed through the leafy screen and discovered such a garden, I scarce dared enter it, it seemed too lovely to desecrate, to tread therein. But after my baptism on the hill, what wonder I drenched my body in the warm sunshine that filled these untrodden dells.

My herb-collecting then took second, third, fourth place, and sometimes no place at all. I could not and would not strip those stately foxgloves of their big lower leaves nor pull the centaury from its slight hold in the leafy mould. It was that I must leave those woodland sanctuaries as I found them, not that I was worried about hurt to the plants. Foxglove is quite unharmed by the taking of its lower leaves. One does not take all; the

I saw without looking

flowers are untouched; the seeds ripen; and provided the new woodland growth does not again become too dense, there will be another splendid array in two years' time. Centaury at first I pulled, for this is much the easiest way to gather it. But I soon saw that by so doing I was likely to remove it from my countryside for good and all, because it is collected just as it comes into full flower and before any seed has formed or had time to scatter. So I went armed with my all-purpose broken table-knife. With this I grew very expert at severing those slender stems just above the root, which I could feel rather than see among the thick growth whence it sprang. It was with great satisfaction that I noticed afterwards that plants thus cut sprouted again and flowered again and their perpetuation was assured.

Centaury was perhaps, at one and the same time, the most delightful and the easiest of all the herbs I collected. Not that it was abundant or even common; I would spend a whole day searching for it and not collect more than a dozen pounds. Being only six to eighteen inches high, it made neat, compact bundles, easy and convenient to handle. And what a perfume there was to it! It was like the scent of fresh tea with something else added, something essentially English, the sweetness and fragrance of the woodlands of this England.

The drying of it was simple. No need to hang it on my drying lines or to spread it out on my shelves of garden netting; all I did was to tie it up in little bundles, a dozen or more on one length of string, for all the world like the tail of a kite, and festoon these about the walls of the cottage. There it hung in nobody's way, taking up no space, scenting the rooms with its delicate perfume. It hung there for weeks, for on account of some oily content it never dried crisp or brittle like most other herbs did. Hence it was bagged up at any time it suited me, and never did I know it to mould. I never made 'centaury tea', said to be good for indigestion, nor attempted any extract or infusion from any of the herbs I collected. At the time I neither believed nor disbelieved in their medicinal qualities, and to say so does not convict me of hypocrisy. I took a pride in gathering and harvesting the very best. I gathered that I might sell. Herbs were needed and what use was made of them I did not know. Nevertheless, I secretly hoped that those who ultimately bought might be benefited thereby. Not that this or that patent medicine might cure their ills, but that the essence of the countryside, its fragrance, its sunshine, its serene, might creep into their hearts and minds. An absurd and extravagant hope perhaps, yet sometimes, when sitting comfortably and sipping my cup of tea, I become aware that it is not just an infusion of the leaves of the tea plant that quenches my thirst and pleases my palate, for I realise that tropical sun and monsoon rains, mountain slopes and ancient soil, toiling hands and patient care, are distilled in the fragrant steam that coils in rainbow vapours from my cup; and I am thankful for all that, and stimulated thereby. If such qualities do not attach to mundane things we might as well not live. The ethics of herbs and medicine worried me not at all while I lived at Copsford. Since then, however, I have wondered why anyone believing in medicine at all should discriminate between one source of extract and another.

In overgrown rides and tangled clearings where brambles grew unchecked and thrust barbed runners as snares for the unwary through weeds and grasses, and where in June and July their white, multi-stamened blossoms attracted myriads of insects, there I met and made friends with lovely butterflies. Few things delight my eyes quite so much as the sight and flight of the white admiral. Butterflies are so closely associated in our minds with rich and brilliant colours that black and white might seem sober dress for the white admiral. Indeed, it would be were it not for two things: that the undersides of the wings are a lovely mottled pattern of russet, grey and white, and that the white coincides with the white bars of the upper surface, thus giving a marvellous effect of brilliant transparency as the butterfly glides and glances through woodland sunshine. In my boyhood a white admiral was the rarest of rare insects. One caught in Sussex would have been regarded with almost more wonder and delight than a Camberwell beauty: that famous insect of all boyish hearts-desiring. It was to be found only locally in woods of western England, and never did we go so far as western Sussex. But this aristocrat of butterflies has done a remarkable thing. It suddenly expanded its restricted boundaries; it left its hereditary home, its blue blood flowed more freely, its numbers increased enormously. It reached Wiltshire, Hampshire, Berkshire. It reached Sussex. When I lived in Copsford in July I frequently saw it, and I was filled with the same joy and excitement that would have stirred me years before by the sight of something so choice and so full of grace. Since then the white admiral has become even more abundant. Recently I have seen a score or more in one short walk through a Sussex wood and I cannot help wondering what conditions made it possible for this butterfly to spread so amazingly. Most butterflies show a very marked tendency to remain close to the spot where, as caterpillars, they were born and bred. With some species localities are confined to a few acres. This might often be accounted for by the extent of a peculiar food plant. But in the case of the white admiral the food plant is the common wild honeysuckle, a plant which is abundant over the whole of England. Was a sport suddenly born in which the homing instinct was nonexistent or displaced by an urge to rove? Or did its larvae or pupae suddenly escape the attentions of some parasitic ichneumon fly? Or did it suddenly cease to be the peculiar food for some ordinary bird? Or could there have been some special quality about the honeysuckle of western England without which it could not thrive until by some accident a brood was successfully reared on a more ordinary kind? The puzzle is not yet solved and my only fear is that we may not discover the solution until the wheel comes full circle and the very causes, or their converse, which allowed the insect to increase, will once again restrict it to its original localities.

Look at the superb insect as it glances through the sunbeams and shadows of an untrodden woodland ride. The effortless grace of its flight, the luminous countercharge on its sable wings, make it appear as though sunlight only were the medium of its flight. It speeds and glides and skims about the oaks and sweet-chestnut clumps, vanishes in the shadows, reappears in the dazzling sunshine above the bramble blossoms, floats here, beats vigorously there, settles lightly on a truss of bloom and supping the nectar with rapidly darting tongue, off again to poise for a few seconds on sun-warmed leaf, then away among the oaks to do battle with the purple hairstreak or others of its kind, and on and on through the sun-long day till the shadows fill the blossoms. Who would not count himself fortunate to number such a sprite among his friends?

And the silver-washed fritillary, what can I say of that dashing gallant of the butterfly nobility? It has such rich associations; the blazing July sun, the strong, warm smell of vigorous bracken, the hum of laden bees, boyish triumph above bare and bloody knees, golden days in carefree years. So much is bound up with its buoyant, bold flight, its tigerish wings – tawny-orange and black, the choice silver on the underside of its hind wings, like sea-washed silver sand on a green-weed carpet – that I find myself at a loss to set any but a fraction of it all down. As I think about the silver-washed fritillary my pen dries, poised above the paper. I stare away into the sunny vistas of the past. I see long rides and massed bramble blossom. I see open clearings with tall plume thistles. I see foxglove and centaury. I see trees, great trees, trysting trees, where eyes meet and hands clasp, and the fritillaries speed silently by.

There was one tree, a beech, that I particularly loved. It had a girth of about twenty feet and was probably the sole survivor of the destruction caused by the urgent demand for ships and cannon to destroy Napoleon. How far-reaching are the repercussions of the acts of would-be world dictators. How came it about, I mused, that this one tree should have been saved? Did a charcoal-burner have romantic fancies about this beech? I imagined him crudely carving the initials of his sweetheart on the glossy bole of the tree under which they had so often met. Had the dreaded name of 'Boney' cast a shadow across their rustic courting and a strange fate compelled him to fell the very forest where they had so often met? Somehow he had contrived to save this one tree. Perhaps she had been its saviour by urging him never to permit the tree which bore her name to be burned and cast into the furnace to smelt base iron.

Was this broad ancient scar A for Ann or J for Joan? Was the name of Nelson whispered here, and did the news of Waterloo bring the lovers to rejoice again beneath this very tree? Time has borne them all away. They are forgotten; only the beech stands lord of all, and neither Kaiser nor corporal can bring it down.

After I had discovered the great beech I took the music mistress to see it, and we sat in the great spread of its shade, and listened to the rustle of the wind as it whispered in the beech leaves. Squirrels came and nibbled the beech mast, and a fox trotted lightly down the opposite bank to drink at a streamlet. We scarcely said a word until, when about to leave, I drew her attention to the few legible initials carved in the massive trunk. She liked them.

'"Fools",' I said, '"like their faces, put their names in public places"; that's what my elder brother taught me when he went to boarding school.'

She laughed gaily, saying that some irate schoolmaster must have taught him that for cutting his name in the classroom wall. 'Anyway, this isn't a public place, is it?'

No, it was not. And I visited it again, alone, very soon afterwards, while fritillaries still skimmed about me and foxgloves were in blossom.

AGRIMONY

THE AGRIMONY CROP kept me very busy. Because the fields about Copsford were rough and unkempt pastures, or with wide and ragged edges and hedges, this herb was everywhere common. The more I searched for it the greater grew my surprise at its abundance. Although eighteen inches to three feet high, it is not a conspicuous plant. Usually growing in coarse grasses, its slender spike of yellow blossom rarely rises much above them. It springs from a rosette of quite large, hairy, somewhat sticky-feeling leaves, and its stem is hollow but tough. Glancing casually into a rough unmown pasture from the tumble-down bar-way you might say that there was no agrimony there at all. Purple knapweed, yes, abundant, and dyers' greenweed as showy as you like, thistle too conspicuous, but *Agrimonia eupatoria* seemingly absent. Enter the field and you unexpectedly notice a spike about three yards from the hedge. You walk towards it and spot two other plants quite near. Much surprised you wonder why you did not see them from the bar-way, and looking back, to your astonishment, you now see that you have just walked past another, and there is another, and another. Agrimony is like that. It is right under your nose when you are looking for it three yards in front. Of course there are other places where it grows as conspicuous as hollyhocks in the herbaceous border, but as a rule it is shy and retiring. I had to cultivate its acquaintance. I had to train myself to observe and, when I began to see it I saw it in hundreds and thousands.

It is strange how the unobservant eye is bemused by size and colour. Of teazles growing along a stretch of riverbank you might say there were hundreds, where in actual fact there would only be a few score. Walking along a woodland path in autumn you would say that you had seen a few toadstools, yet if you had really used your eyes you might have seen dozens of many colours, sorts and sizes. On a background of greens and straw and browns it is purples and mauves and blues that stand conspicuous. In autumn woods when russet and bronze, sienna and madder, richly paint the underwood, even the scarlet fly agaric is easily overlooked by the casual observer.

How careless we are about the training of our eyes to perceive colour. Day in, day out, year in, year out, what joy do we experience in the perception of exquisite colours? Only once did I ever meet a man who suggested that I should get up early one morning, as he had done on several occasions, to see colour, to see the light of the rising sun play on a particular tiled roof. It was a somewhat steeply falling roof, facing north, and only at certain seasons of the year did the morning sun glance warmly across it. Then it glowed and smouldered like the embers of a wood fire swept by the wind, with blue and violet, purple and orange flames darting about it.

Were not most of us brought up with the impression that colour and its appreciation was the province of artists alone? As young children we found much pleasure in playing with our paintboxes. How well I remember some of the amazing colours my elder brother produced from the hard rubbing-paints out of my grandfather's Victorian paintbox. They were used to colour the little paper figures of Admiral Benbow and Captain Shufflebottom, and other pirates that played on the tiny stage of our toy theatre. I shall never forget the vivid headgear of those romantic sailors, nor the sumptuous, low-cut rainbow gowns of the heroine.

But we grow up. For most of us the paintbox becomes a childish thing and it is never brought out again. We lose interest in colour. Occasionally we decide on a scheme for our sitting-room furniture, or the mixture of our tailor-made. Once or twice in the year we are surprised at the pleasure we experience in the sight of a rose or an apple, but it rarely occurs to us that we should find as much delight in the world of colour as in the world of music. We blunder along wearing the dark-blue spectacles of indifference and preoccupation, 'we have not time to stand and stare'. For me, however, while at Copsford, this was not true. I had plenty of time, and at first I did not know how to use it. Making a living, the struggle to make ends meet, the rush and hustle of city life, the never-ending round of daily tasks, the squirrels' cage, gets us so wound up that we find ourselves incapable of rest and contemplation. If we try we feel guilty of idling, we are wasting precious time, we ought to be doing this or preparing that. We ought to be knitting or writing, or preparing the meal, or ordering tomorrow's. We ought to he mowing the lawn, or darning the socks, or phoning the secretary, or planning the next war.

But at Copsford there were seasons when time almost stood still, and I too learnt to be still. At first I was restless, miserable, a gnawing discontent tried to eat my heart out, and if I had not been blessed with an inborn love of the countryside it would have succeeded. But I slowly learned to stand and stare. The leaven was working. I not only stood and not only stared, but I began to see. I saw lovely things and rare things, quaint and curious things, colours, marvellous and surpassing the imagination of the proudest paintbox in the world, saw the play of light across meadow and wood, saw a shaft of sunlight fill a spring-green copse till it glowed as though the glory of the Light of the World dwelled within. I caught an occasional glimpse of the intricate and complex pattern of life, and once or twice, as fleeting as the rainbow-flash from a trembling dewdrop, I perceived that all these things were but the external signs of a kingdom such as I had never dreamed of; that these colours were as a drop-curtain which, while it might never rise to disclose the stage within, grew transparent before my wondering eyes.

At first I cut agrimony with a knife, but soon found that by doing so I was losing the rosette of large leaves at the foot of the stem. It was important that I should gather these, for the whole plant is used by the herbalists, often in the preparation of a cough cure, and there was much goodness in the leaves. From my point of view, also, these leaves were important, for they added enormously to the weight of the gathering. In fact a bundle of stems only would weigh fifteen pounds.

Agrimony stems are very tough, they cannot be snapped off; but I soon found that a sharp, firm pull would break the stem two or three inches below the surface and then I had all the large leaves, several dried and decayed ones as well, beside the extra length of stem. This well-nigh quadrupled the weight and made my in-going tally quite imposing. But such whole-hog methods had some unpleasant results. The picking out of the dead, dried and rotten leaves was tedious and time-wasting, and the root stem dried such a bad colour that I often had to cut it off. The pulling of this tough plant rubbed my fingers sore. I can imagine the amusement this will cause to the horny-handed folk who have gloried in outdoor toil all their lives, but the fact remains that my hands became so sore that I just could not go on, partly no doubt because my hands were still soft from the city, partly because performing the same vigorous action over and over again, hundreds and hundreds of times, was bound to rub the weakest place sore. Lastly, after nearly a month had gone by since the first cutting, I was amazed to discover, on going over old ground, that where I had first used the knife the agrimony plants had sprouted vigorously again, two, three and even four stems; I could start all over again and gather a yet heavier crop from the same ground. To my dismay I discovered that where I had pulled the agrimony there were no shoots, no plants at all.

Going the whole hog never does pay in the long run, so I returned to the knife, cutting below the rosette wherever I could, and had the satisfaction of reaping a double harvest wherever I did so.

The change to the open fields, after the secrecy and seclusion of the woods, was great. My every movement was laid bare to the world. Man, bird and beast could observe me and gossip about my doings. For a week or two I was uncomfortable and felt all the time that I was being watched and all my actions became absurdly self-conscious. I would often look up sharply to see who was watching, but I never caught sight of a man. Birds and beasts, yes, and reptiles and insects, they were all around me and filled with curiosity, but never a human being. At first I thought mankind mighty cunning, but gradually, very gradually, I realised that there really was nobody, I had these one or two square miles of waste country to myself.

A remarkable sense of freedom pervaded my being.

Every common custom, every irksome convention, fell from me like broken fetters. Mind and body were free. To be released from every worry and care, how few can attain that nowadays. I don't claim to have lived in that blessed state during the whole of my sojourn at Copsford – far from. it – but there were days together, golden days, when nothing worried me and I was anxious about nothing for the morrow. I was my own master. Time meant little, and meals I ate how and when I pleased.

I scarcely remember using watch or clock during the whole of that summer. Like the wildlife around me I obeyed the light, and by so doing began to understand for the first time what a powerful influence it was. Or rather, reversing the point of view, the remarkable response made by all living things to varying intensities of light. If the morning were dull and heavy, then Floss and I woke late. What scraps of breakfast there were, bread and butter, tea and dog biscuits, we partook leisurely, Floss frequently taking a piece out of the front door to toss playfully or bury in a grass tussock. The dandelions by the doorstep were still tight-closed, the wood owl hooted once or twice from ivy-covered oaks behind the cottage. There was not the song and activity among the small birds. The rousing of all life was quiet and slow.

The liveliness of a bright morning was astonishing. Floss would often wake me before the sun crept under my eyelids. She would leap on the bed, lick my face vigorously, leap down again, run to the door, then patter under the bed and perhaps scratch noisily at the rat-blockaded skirting. If all this failed to move me, she would yap and up on the bed again with more strenuous licking. We hurried with the breakfast, I grew impatient with the primus. How slowly the kettle boiled! I would over-pump the thing and there would be a hiss and a geyser of paraffin would burst into flame, reaching the ceiling. Fumes and oily black smoke poured out of the door and up the stairs. I would race round the table to turn the air tap, and Floss, catching the excitement, would tear after me, and out of the front door, and round and round the cottage yapping as though the devil were biting her behind. While the air cleared in the cottage I would join her and she would come and stand with me on the hilltop, nose in air, the breeze just lifting her ears, and we would take stock of those wonderful summer mornings. She used her nose, her ears and, to a lesser degree, her eyes. I used my eyes and ears but my nose scarcely at all. Everything was astir. The bird music before the sun rose was especially lovely. In those quiet expectant minutes the blend of their varied voices had the quality of many-stringed instruments. Except for a solo blackbird or thrush, the hilltop was quiet, but from either side, from the course of the Darn, where bushes, hedgerows and copse abutted on the stream, I could distinguish separate choirs of voices. It was the selfsame music that has always lifted my heart, ever since the days when as a lad I heard it rising from a gorse-filled combe in the Southdown country.

Before the sun rose, that is before the intensity of light reached its first climax, the birdsong almost ceased, and where before bird life had been still, it now expressed itself in movement. Birds left the cover of woods or bushes for the marsh or the open pasture to find food. Duck and snipe changed their feeding grounds. The heron came beating slowly upstream to find a favourite reach for fish, and lapwings began half-timid, half-aggressive antics when they saw him. Floss spotted a cock pheasant as it ran behind a hedge towards the Darn. She longed to race after it, but she was too obedient to move without my command. A few minutes later the cock must have reached its crowing pitch, for we heard its clarion and the queer drumming of the wings which instantly followed. A woodpecker came down on the pasture to search for ants, and I saw that a pair of cole tits had already commenced their unceasing search for grubs for the family of seven, safely housed in the hollow of a rotten stump near my bathing-pool.

But while increasing light stirred many to vigorous activity, on some creatures its influence was the reverse. The brown wood owl had soon been driven to his ivy, the little, so-called Dutch, owl had long ceased to worry the moorhens by suddenly pouncing down on beetles among the rush tussocks. Badgers vanished at the first hint of a brilliant morning, and bats could not endure rapid increase in intensity of light.

Of course the nocturnal activity of such creatures as bats and little owls is largely governed by the food for which they search. That, in large part, is insect life, and the specialised part on which they feed is itself nocturnal, or at least crepuscular; beetles and moths, for example. There are, however, myriads of insects which provide food for other creatures during daylight hours, and which could well feed the bats. But whether the nocturnal animals have schooled themselves to shun the light, or simply do so so that they may catch the food they prefer, the whole point is that it is the intensity of light which controls their movements. They are not conscious of the passage of time as men understand it, but they are amazingly sensitive to light. This sensitivity is not necessarily through the eyes; earthworms, for example, are sensitive at their extremities but not in their middle section, and they certainly have no eyes.

As Floss and I watched the sunrise, I did not then think of all these things. I was simply conscious of the power of light and the response that I was making to it. It was an almost unconscious response. I did not leave my bed because of time – because it was 'time to get up'. I rose because it was light. The light woke me, drew me, in a measure fascinated me. Was there, is there, some hidden interplay, some unknown interaction, between light and the body, or light and the mind, or all three?

It is good for us sometimes to wonder. Without imagination the light that is in us may well be darkness. And it is a fact that during those summer months at Copsford, when I was oppressed by no anxieties or worries, when no evil bore me down, when I lived to the full every carefree hour, when perhaps my eye was single, it was then that light had its strongest hold upon me. Do not we take light too much for granted? Is not light the only chain that links universe to universe at last?

Because Floss and I rose early to greet the sun on those happy summer mornings, it must not be thought that I was one of those unbelievable persons who can always spring on waking, from their beds, fresh and energetic. In those Copsford days it was natural; it would have been unthinkable, impossible, to lie in bed with the July sun rising high in the heavens. Since then, I am as bad as ever, and though I know it would be delicious to be up and out and feel the sun stream level across the countryside, yet my response to light is so sluggish that there I lie. Only while on holiday do I sometimes react naturally, and perhaps climb mountains in the half-light before dawn that I may see the sunrise on those beloved fells, and feel the onrush and intensity of unfolding light. Perhaps the secret of perfect rest lies in a carefree mind; and given both, one is no doubt receptive to unusual and maybe unknown influences.

Fading light had the reverse effect upon me. The setting sun hurried me back to the cottage. I did not care to sit up after dark and read or write. I only had candlelight for illumination, but if I had had the best lamplight in the village it could have made no difference. I became uneasy and unsettled, I was too restless to concentrate on anything. I caught myself taut, staring at the uneasily bobbing candle flame, ears a-cock for the least sound, within or without. Floss and I were not happy till we went upstairs, she to lie at the foot of the bed, I to snuff the candle, slip off my clothes in the moonlight, and creep satisfied into bed, happy indeed to shut my eyes till light should prise them open.

Out in the agrimony fields I made the acquaintance of many insects. They were not the aristocratic butterflies of the woodlands, but a host of horseflies, bees, burnet moths, skippers, meadow browns, blues, coppers, tortoiseshells, common flies, stinging flies, dung flies and a hundred others. The horseflies I grew to dislike very much. After my discovery that I was alone in that empty countryside I often discarded my shirt altogether and went clad only in shorts, with a knotted handkerchief for my head. This exposed me to the merciless attacks of the horseflies, and some sunny days I was hard put to it to decide whether or not to wear a shirt. It was so delightful to feel the warmth of sun on my back and the play of the breeze about my body, that any covering was irksome, yet on certain days the horseflies were so persistent, so determined to settle on my back and have my blood, that I was driven nearly silly trying to ward off their attacks.

I noticed two kinds: there were the big fellows, more than an inch long and stout in proportion, which made a deep, surly humming as they approached. For all their size they were very timid and one swish of my switch was enough to send them streaking, for while they seemed slow and sluggish when approaching their quarry, they were, normally, speedy on the wing; they troubled me very little. It was the smaller species that molested me most. They were barely half the size of their big relations, slender, with greyish wings, which folded along the sides of their bodies, bulging eyes, two short, sinister-looking antennae, and a cruel-looking, downward-pointing 'beak'. They were almost silent on the wing, and amid all the noises of midsummer hum I could never hear their approach. These horseflies had a most uncanny way of always attacking from behind. It was always on the back of my legs, behind my knees, on my back and on the back of my arms and neck, that they settled. These wretched insects didn't 'bite' at once, they paused, they seemed to take stock of the boundless meal spread before them, perhaps they gained confidence. Then almost invariably they would move a few steps, select what I suppose was to them the ideal spot, and then slowly and cautiously press that awl-shaped proboscis close to the flesh, cunningly and very rapidly make the incision, and then pretty well bury their faces in the flesh. The extraordinary thing was that this was usually done so stealthily that I was often not aware that I had been bitten until the insect withdrew its knife. This I felt, and struck, usually too late, for the wretch had either buzzed drunkenly away, or let go its hold and fallen, with blood-distended abdomen, among the grasses.

A little red puncture was left in the skin, which sometimes developed into an irritable bump. But it was not the after-effects so much as the cunning, stealthy attack that made me detest them. Where they were very numerous and persistent I often tried walking backwards, attempting to deceive them and to make them attack where I could see them and strike them down with my switch, or else to observe where they settled on my flesh and then slap them flat against my naked body. This ruse sometimes succeeded; but for uncanny intelligence I hand it to the horsefly.

As is the case with most flies, they had their pestiferous days and their off days. On some bright days I was not molested at all; on other days, equally sunny and bright, their thirst for blood knew no bounds. I could never be certain what the conditions were that determined when they were biting, but there is no doubt that sultry, thundery weather increased their activity. Although I carried a switch of leafy hazel or hornbeam, or fronds of bracken, and used it as continuously as a cow her tail, I must admit I got into the habit of taking my shirt with me, hung in my belt, and donning it when the pests were most tiresome.

But it must not be thought that my days were made a misery by these horseflies and other stinging flies. They were incidental, just the flies in the ointment. They were not in every pasture or rough meadow where I gathered agrimony. More often than not they infested the low-lying fields near the Darn, and smaller areas shut in by wood and copse. Up on higher ground, where there was less water and more breeze, I scarcely saw them. They were never active until the sun was high, and during cloudy, overcast weather they remained hidden.

Wherever I went collecting agrimony, butterflies abounded. They were the common kinds to be found about any flowery meadow, yet to me every butterfly, however ordinary, is a source of pleasure and delight; and of course I include moths. My constant companion was the meadow brown, a butterfly quiet in hue and appearing clumsy in flight, and so abundant that every schoolboy scorns it. It thrives on neglect; waste fields, untended and unknown pastures; these are its happy homes. It does not seem to have been marked down as the particular food for any bird. It does not rank in carefully, proudly tended rows in the entomologist's cabinet, for it sports no valuable variations and is rarely subject to striking aberrations. Perhaps if we had to climb mountains to high alpine pastures, as we do to catch a glimpse of its cousin, the mountain ringlet, before we could find the meadow brown, we might value it more highly; we might even risk life and limb in mad chase down the fell side to triumph in its capture when we closed the lid of the killing-bottle upon it. But it is common, it is neglected, it lives. Even then, how it survives in such numbers makes me wonder, for it is one of the butterflies which live the winter through as a small caterpillar. The last summer brood lays its eggs in August and September. These eggs hatch and, after a short period of grass feeding, the little caterpillars crawl away to find winter quarters, and all through the long six months of hibernation a score of dangers beset them. There are hungry birds, hungry mice, moles, beetles, centipedes; there are tramping cattle, and floods, and human activities, there are frosts and suffocating snows; and I suppose countless thousands of larvae succumb. But nature is so prodigal in her expenditure of life in order that a few may live, that always enough win through to the warm days of spring to feed once again on tender young grasses, to pass the pupal stage girded to a stem, to emerge in June a common meadow brown. Who would not love so triumphant, so modest an adventurer?

Then there were the skippers; they were a merry crew. I had met Dingy and Grizzled when I was gathering clivers; they played about in odd waste corners, never flying far, never flying fast, but flitted, skipped, so inconspicuously to and fro amid the withered stems of the previous year's luxuriance, that whenever I felt not quite sure whether or not I had seen a butterfly, I could be pretty certain that I had, and that it was a skipper.

The grizzled skipper was a favourite; it has wings a miniature chequer-hoard of black and white, and a daintily charged margin. Half a dozen of them played catch-me-if-you-can, and skipped to home on the dry, withered heads of knapweed or amongst the sharp, brittle bracken, where they rested, wings wide, and let the sun play 'mate in two moves.

At agrimony-time it was the small and the large skipper that played many tricks with my eyes among the flowers. The new bracken was tall and green and unrolled by then, and the knapweeds had new purple heads of blossom. Both these skippers had a queer way, when resting sunning on a flower head, of setting their wings at half cock, for they neither close them over their backs nor spread them wide to the sun, but hold them curiously separated and on edge, as if they wanted the breeze between them as well as the sunshine upon them.

Perhaps no moth gave me more pleasure, as a child, than the six-spot burnet, and then it was not so much the perfect insect, gorgeous as that was in its glossy, metallic blue-black sheen with crimson spots and crimson underwings, as the fascinating cocoon which enclosed the chrysalis that appealed so strongly to my childish imagination. Wherever the six-spot makes its home, which is certainly not everywhere, for it is particular about its choice, it is abundant, and one can see in the early summer these lovely golden, sometimes silvery, cocoons spun delicately each on a single grass stem. The unpractised eye might not notice them easily, for they harmonise wonderfully with the strawy stems of the grasses, but if the sun is low, shining from behind as we walk across a burnet meadow, then indeed we shall see one, two, a dozen, scores, glistening in the level light.

They have an added attraction to a child because they are so simple to gather. Caterpillars and chrysalises easily squash in clumsy, unthinking fingers, but a burnet cocoon can be taken by simply plucking a single grass stem, and no hurt or damage come to it. How it intrigued me that a caterpillar could produce that glossy waterproof wrapping and still remain inside. What did happen within? How could a caterpillar change into a sheeny moth with wings? How could it get out? And when I had them home, a little bouquet in a jam jar, I was still further fascinated by the rustling sounds which came from within. What were they doing inside those silken hammocks? For it is a fact that six-spot burnet larvae and the chrysalises are most restless within their cocoons. It is not possible to hear their movements out of doors, at least I have never noticed it, but indoors, in the quiet of a child's bedroom, it was at times insistent and curious to listen to. Whatever were they doing? Could they not get out? Were they talking to each other? Were they stirring in their sleep?

They were jolly insects on the wing, shockingly late risers, it is true, often not starting the day's business till the sun was high in the sky, but quite fearless. They were fond of each other's company, crowding half a dozen on a single thistle head, and in no hurry to leave. When they did, it was to zoom by as if their heavy, plushy bodies were too much for their narrow wings, and I could often see their great club-hooked antennae, held erect like horns, as they hurried past. An aura of crimson seemed to envelop them as they flew. I was sorry when they were no longer with me.

But I had many other winged companions which, like the meadow browns, seemed with me all the summer long, because they were double and sometimes treble brooded. They were the coppers and the blues. What burnished brilliance there was in the wings of those small coppers! I sometimes caught myself wishing they were ten times their size, say ten inches across the wings. How they would startle the landscape! But it must never be, for once, less than a hundred years ago, we did have a copper only half as large again as the small, with burnished wings unsullied by a single dusky spot or mourning band, and it has gone; it is lost, irretrievably. What else is there so tragic as the loss of a life form that can never, never reappear? I know it has happened hundreds, more probably thousands of times in the past; creatures have, as it were, taken the wrong turning, to find themselves in a blind alley from which there is no retreat, only extinction. Changing climate and physical conditions have, slowly or suddenly, wiped out legions of living creatures as completely and with the same finality as I rub chalk figures from the slate that records my agrimony tally. The dust blows out of the open door.

Barely three miles from Copsford is a clay pit. It was there, to the astonishment of all, that fossils were found, beyond the least shadow of doubt, of the iguanodon, giant, kangaroo-like reptile of the Jurassic and Cretaceous ages. It makes one tremble to touch these cold, stony links with the tremendous past; and how the imagination leaps to create pictures of that monstrous beast, sploshing cumbrously in the muddy waters of a mighty delta, whose river no man ever saw, whose course no man has ever known. Here in Sussex, where there is now the clayey Weald and the chalk hills, was a fantastic world where these very things were in the making. The slimy muds, poured into that ancient sea by the unknown Amazon, were to become the clays of London and southeastern England. Already in that sea inconceivable trillions of foraminifera, two thousand to the inch, had commenced to form the reefs that were to become the chalk downs. Jungles of ferns, horsetails, reeds and conifers covered the marshland. Dinosaurs and plesiosaurs joined the iguanodon, pterodactyls flapped overhead; yet somewhere in that grotesque world the first mammals were developing, the first true birds were flying, the first of modern trees began to flourish, insects were numerous.

The last iguanodon died; the huge, thirty-foot body sank in the mud, and of his bones were fossils made. One wakes with a jerk; why, the very bricks which build our houses, which built Copsford, are from that world and bear traces of that life. So the iguanodon rears its head again where it did such long ages past.

The extinction of such ancient and fearful life forms we can be truly thankful for, but it comes as something of a shock that the large copper butterfly, on the wing within living memory, is as extinct as those monsters of the Cretaceous age. No fenland mud could enshrine the tiny corpse to be converted in future ages to a delicate fossil. There was no resinous sap to trap and entomb the insect so that it might be seen by generations yet to come as a fly in amber. No, only in a few cabinets are there some pinned and labelled specimens, worth maybe more than fifty times their weight in gold, that must, as the brief centuries hurry by, come to dust. Then will the large copper be less familiar than the pterodactyl. It is a tragedy, for it might have been on the wing today had but a few acres of fenland been reserved, or the vicious collector been restrained. But the busy Victorians were too busy, and we awoke to our loss too late, for the last large copper must have flashed by in the sun before the dawn of the twentieth century. We have, it is true, tried to make amends. We have introduced the continental large copper, we have reserved a fen for its well-being and it thrives. That is good news indeed. I hope it spreads far and wide; it will be a sign of these astonishingly contradictory times.

So, my little copper, I am glad you are no larger. I am glad you are as common as my meadow browns, nobody wants the halfpence except the schoolboys.

Well, what a long way we have wandered to gather agrimony! My back is burnt red and brown and chocolate. It aches from continual stooping. My fingers are sore. I stagger under the burden of two huge bundles. The sweet, honey-lemon scent perfumes me from head to foot, it seems to enter my very being, it has become a part of me. The stiff spikes of pale golden-yellow blossom now droop and swing like a hundred grey-gold tassels from each bundle. In time I shall reach Copsford and Floss will greet me and inspect my day's work. We shall weigh the costly bales and I shall chalk up the score. Then I shall unroll the rich merchandise, and soon it will be on the strings, curtain after curtain, grey and silver, red-green and gold, and the fragrance will fill the cottage and steal into my dreams, and the iguanodon will walk again, and the large copper fly out of my grandfather's Victorian paintbox.

TRAVELLER'S JOY

Away to the hills we went with borrowed bicycles; to the hills, to the hills, where the wild thyme blows and the sea sparkles under the August blue. By tarry main and dusty road, by flowery by-lane and meandering stream we sped. Through village suddenly boisterous and busy with bus-loads and charabanc, through hamlets still forgotten in the folds of the hills where the song of our free wheels echoed from the quiet walls, up steep inclines to pant and pause and hear the yellow hammers trill and wheeze along the wires, by rugged sun-baked cart track we passed, till the hills grew bold and tall and steep, rich in light and shadow, bush and fosse and sheep track in strong relief above our heads, the quiet turf beneath our wheels; and there we halted.

Those bicycles we hid in clump of elder and wayfaring tree, all bowered over with traveller's joy, and then we climbed, the music mistress and I, up the face of the steep escarpment. Steep it was, and the grass dry and slippery, and we scrambled and slithered, and I held out my hand to help her up the sharpest bit, and she clung on so suddenly that I almost lost my balance. We might have tobogganed in undignified delight to the bottom again, but we just maintained our equilibrium and scrambled to the ledge of a sheep run. There we sat to gasp for breath.

We listened to the silence, gazing out across the blue distances of the tranquil Weald. The bleat of the flock somewhere on the lower slopes came softened and musical, with a bronze bell pointing the phrases. Far below us was a threshing machine already busy eating up the first stacks, and its queer drone rising and suddenly falling blended unceasingly with the hum of many insects. In the lee of the hill-crest the light sea breeze was baffled and scarce a breath fanned our hot faces, but we could hear its tiny song, above our heads, whispered to the grasses. Away across the plain we followed the white plume of a train, threading its way across the mosaic of field and woodland. How slowly it travelled! Yet for all its rushing and clanking sixty miles an hour, never a sound reached our ears. We listened to the refreshing quiet made wonderful by tiny sounds, the thin quire of a multitude of grasshoppers, a lizard scuttling to its hole, the splitting pods of the gorse.

At length we moved on over the crest of the hill and in one stride the whole paradise of downland burst into view, fold on fold, shadowy combe, shimmering ridge, till they broke abruptly on the sea. And away to left and right they rolled, sweeping onward to Ditchling and the Dyke, rising gently to Firle. No rock, no scree, no crag, no precipice, just tumbling, undulating green grassland where many might roam and never meet.

The sight of the sea made us catch our breath. I do not know what it is with us in England, but the sight of the sea stirs us deeply. However much in love with the woodland, the long heath, the brown furze, sooner or later we shall journey and cry with satisfied delight, 'Thalassa! Look, the Sea!' Whether it be the blue riband beyond the sandy dunes, or the broad deep furrowed in catspaws between the cliffs, or the aerial ocean where islands float above the mountains, we feel richly rewarded; we have seen what is ours, what, as islanders, is in part our heritage.

We stood on the hill-crest, gazing fascinated at the golden pathway that widened to the far horizon. Overhead wheeled the swifts, black crescents of speed. They, I thought, would be flying the pathway perhaps that very day; or would it be the pathway of the moon?

What a fantastic and marvellous thing is migration. We have learnt to scoff at the old idea of swallows plunging into the waters of our ponds and rivers, and hibernating in the mud, and in its place we regard as obvious and commonplace their amazing journey to faraway lands. It is so easy to say that they fly away because there is no insect food for them here in winter. One might easily ask why come here at all when in the lands where they 'winter' insect life teems all the year round. Whey should the swift, latecomer in May, leave in mid-August when both April and September could provide all the food he needs, as indeed those months do for countless house martins and swallows?

And there are more intriguing questions than this. How can a bird know when to leave its winter quarters? What informs it, in the midst of subtropical heat, that spring conditions prevail in the nesting land of its choice? What guides it? What keeps it on its course at night, across featureless waters often in rainstorm and cloud? How does it recognise the district of its birth, returning to the very spot where it was born or where it built its nest the previous season? One could pose many other teasing questions, for bird migration is not just confined to insect-eaters which come north in spring and return south in autumn. There are movements in many directions by many kinds of birds at all seasons. There are the starlings hurrying into the British Isles from the Baltic lands in autumn; the influx of jays, crows and magpies from Europe in winter; the redwings and fieldfares from Scandinavia coming down the chain of islands, Faroes, Orkneys, Shetlands to England; the astounding travels of the Arctic tern which spans the Atlantic from end to end; the extraordinary inflow of millions of sea birds to our coasts in early spring; the countless hosts of warblers and the swallow kind in April and May. There is no end to the travellers and their wonderful journeys; why, it is now known that many of our blackbirds and thrushes take it into their heads to winter in Spain and Portugal.

Take it into their heads, do they? Is it a matter of mind? Is it a matter of protoplasmic activity within the cells? And do we want to know the answers to all these questions? The ornithologist might, the biologist probably would, the psycho-biologist certainly seeks them; but you and I and the music mistress, do the answers concern us? Shall our love for birds be in any way affected by them, however interesting? I think not; we love birds for the life, the vivacious spirit that is expressed in and by them, and we perceive and feel that expression rather than understand it. I recently heard a famous modern musician, in reply to a question on how one could learn to understand music, say that music was not a matter of understanding but of feeling. How heartily I endorse that opinion. I can listen to the music mistress playing a Chopin Etude or Beethoven Sonata and be strangely moved by the poignancy of the melody and the grandeur and intensity of the harmonies, yet know nothing at all about its key, theme, construction or harmony. She knows, for she has made it her work to understand all the technicalities and to master them. But she would be the first to declare that it is quite unnecessary for the listener either to know or to have mastered them. But neither she nor any other musician can tell how it is or why it is a certain sequence of notes or resolving harmonies cause the spine to thrill, the heart to leap, the mind to soar.

Up on the Downs there I could have told her about the swifts and the swallows, the starlings and the terns; how keen and enthusiastic ornithologists both in Britain and abroad have ringed hundreds of thousands of birds of many species with little aluminium 'anklets' bearing identification numbers; how many hundreds of these marked birds have been recovered; how the wonders of their travels have been exactly recorded; how we have learned nearly all the great routes and movements. But no one could tell her why birds migrate, or how they have learned or how they are able to perform their journeys.

But to know or not to know made no difference that August afternoon to our love for the swift, and our wonder and delight in its life, its flight, its crescent speed, the miracle of its migration. Like a lovely tune with a marvellous development, its life was irresistible, and it was a traveller, a traveller across continents and seas, that same sea we saw sparkling beyond the cliffs. Perhaps tomorrow he would be gone, when for eight months he would skim between earth and sky, over town and country, hill and dale, mountain and lake. How much might happen before that little life once again saw the green hills of England.

We walked on regardless of time and distance. That upland turf is a carpet which never seems to weary those who tread it. So short it is, so compact, so springy; and the view and the sea and the distance hypnotised us; and the roll of the hills, fold on fold, lured us on. There should be no end to such travellers' joy.

At length we came to the lip of a deep combe, half filled with shadow, where we sat and looked down its long hollowed length towards a gap in Downland where a Wealden river flowed. One felt something of the joy of a bird to be poised there on the brink of the wind. It seemed one only had to lean forward with arms outstretched to be buoyed up, and soar and glide, and soar again, till one reached the clouds. A kestrel came over and showed us how to do it; with wonderful wing control it hung for a few seconds poised above our heads, almost motionless, just a tremble in wings and tail; then, dissatisfied, it broke its invisible moorings and allowed the uprushing breeze to carry it higher yet, soaring and sailing into the blue. It was a wonderful object lesson, and I remembered how as children my brothers and sisters and I had delighted to stand on the edge of the sea wall and lean daringly into the salty sou'wester, hanging with outstretched arms at a sharp angle over the seeming depths of the beach below. We never soared, but sometimes we fell or jumped into the abyss, just to have the delight for those brief fractions of a second of hurtling through the air. No serious harm came to us, and I suppose the beach was nothing like so far down as it seemed to us children. Perhaps the force of the wind helped to check our falls, but indeed how rarely do accidents happen to children in carefree play; only when spite and wilfulness and horseplay enter do troubles arise. But the music mistress told me that one hot summer day, when as a little girl she was walking along near the edge of the promenade, she fainted suddenly, and, falling from the wall to the beach below, broke her wrist.

The breeze up the combe brought the scent of many flowers, thyme and bedstraw, campion and scabious, thistle and knapweed, and a hundred others. It was a paradise for butterflies. There were silver-spotted skippers, close relations of those other skippers which played jokes with my eyes in the agrimony fields. They are listed a somewhat rare butterfly, but up there they seemed abundant enough, playing the old game of catch-me-if-you-can, with the heads of the ground thistle for 'home'. There were graylings, butterflies which have for me most mixed associations, because, for some absurd reason, they always suggest stewed gooseberries (I think it must be on account of the soft-coloured eye-spots on the wings), and yet at the same time are rich in memories of high places, of heaths, of rocks, of sunny days. It has most remarkable coloration on the underside of the hind wings, and takes full advantage of the fact, for it plays an even more cunning game than the skippers; perhaps because it usually lives in exposed breezy places and hourly risks being swept away from its native heath. This butterfly is not often of its own choice on the wing, but, when disturbed, it seems to rise like dust before our clumsy feet, and, making full use of following wind, flies speedily a dozen yards or so, when it drops suddenly on a bare or barren patch and vanishes. We creep up cautiously, knowing to within a yard where it has settled, but we simply cannot detect it, its protective resemblance, its camouflage, is so perfect. Where is it? At last we despair, thinking perhaps we had misjudged the distance. We move less cautiously and in an instant it springs again from our astonished feet to play the same trick all over again. On the rare occasions when we can exclaim 'I spy' we notice a strange thing, for the grayling is not settled in the usual manner of a butterfly with its wings closed vertically above its back, but has allowed itself to fall sideways so that only the underside of one hind wing is uppermost, and there is little or no shadow to betray it in relief.

We cannot but marvel at such behaviour which year by year the grayling inherits, and has done, we suppose, for centuries. The butterfly was not taught, it was not shown, it cannot even be aware, as we understand awareness, of the protective coloration of its hind wings, yet every grayling born, we believe, must behave in exactly the same way; if it did not it would not be a grayling. Yet at some remote time the peculiar characteristic must have developed. Was it a sudden sport of behaviour which was so effective in disguising this butterfly from its special enemies, or did the trait evolve, infinitely slowly, from one or more remote ancestors which had a habit of resting ever so slightly out of the vertical? One's imagination reels to think of such a selective process, whereby those butterflies which first displayed this tendency survived death just that little longer than those which had it not, and thus it was more likely that generations of graylings were begotten with it than without it. Thirty thousand generations since the last Ice Age seem scarcely long enough. Perhaps it was much longer. How long must we allow for the astounding cycle: egg, caterpillar, chrysalis, winged insect? Yet what is time in the evolution of an idea and its expression in life? We are so hidebound by our notion of time that there seems no escape from it. Yet surely in the story of creation it is no more than the imaginary flight of time in a book, which can be lightly read, turning the chapters page by page, or left standing on the shelf still with the same record of events set forth within and yet no one conscious of it. We seem to be laboriously reading our world's history, age by age. I wonder if elsewhere in the cosmos our story is complete, standing on the shelves of eternity.

I was roused from my musing by an exclamation from my companion, and saw, at her direction, fluttering towards us up the combe, a new butterfly. It was conspicuous at quite a distance, for not only was it yellow, but making good use of a following wind, it was speeding along at an uphill pace that would have beaten the fastest lad with a net. By happy chance a wayward clump of lucerne checked this joyous traveller and for a few moments we had a close-up of one of the most distinguished of our summer residents – the clouded yellow. What a grand colour for a butterfly: saffron-yellow with deep chocolate tips and bands, and with orange spots, golden sunshine and shadow cloud from the warm south. Could any child wish for a gayer dream come true?

But it was off and away over the crest of the Downs, perhaps to sport in high places, perhaps to descend to the distant Weald, to startle the youthful entomologist into a mad chase, perhaps to return to the sweet-scented clover fields where it was born and bred. Because almost certainly a clouded yellow in August is the offspring of clouded yellows which came to the clover fields of downland in the late spring. Yes, that is indeed the surprising truth, the saffrons are travellers too, travellers from southern Europe, travellers from North Africa, travellers across the sea.

The time had come when we must descend and return to the Weald ourselves. The sun was off the sea, and being well and low to westward, all the north escarpment of the hills was moulded in winsome and fascinating relief. They were so smooth, so soft, of such tender texture, of such exquisite gradation of light and shade, that one could only gaze, and caress with gazing, such loveliness.

We found our bicycles safely where we had hid them among the wayfaring trees and beneath the traveller's joy. And then I remembered that the ostensible reason for our journey had been to pick the leaves of this very plant, *Clematis vitalba*. Sometimes we call it old man's beard, and in late autumn when the cooling sun shines through the silvery plumes of thousands of quaint radial seed heads, the name is good, for the shrubs and trees and bushes seem at a distance hung with age's snow. But more often traveller's joy is the name we give it, and truly it is a name to linger on.

It had so happened that I had received a request for a pound or two of the leaves of this herb, fresh, and it had been a good excuse to ask the music mistress to join me in an expedition to seek and gather some. And there it was at the very end and beginning, not only of our journey, but of many other joyous travellers. As we looked back at the purpling hills we could see the outlines of a colossal figure scored on the face of the down. Each outstretched arm held a pilgrim's staff, and we were reminded, almost as if we heard the music of a Brahms' legend, of that cavalcade out of the dim past of those who journeyed, journeyed towards the quaint sign carved on the bare hill, at whose foot the warm welcome of a priory awaited them; and as they drew near every tree and bush was overhung with traveller's joy.

MEADOWSWEET AND TANSY

Floss taught me many things, but most of all she encouraged me to make full use of my nose. She herself was constantly lifting her soft wet nose to the wind and sniffing delicately. They were not big clumsy single sniffs, such as you and I coarsely make when we think the milk may have boiled over, but innumerable slight sensitive intakes. To her, many small samples were far more effective than single gulps, just as a tea-taster only sips from his miniature cups. Her nose was a study to watch. When one instructs children in something that calls for just a little mental reasoning, as for example one of the less obvious theorems in geometry, because this therefore that, and, as this equals this therefore that equals that, etc, one can see from their eyes whether the children have followed the reasoning and grasped the conclusion. I have heard it argued that there is no expression in the human eyes, that they do not flash or do anything else of that kind which the excited novelist would have us believe. Be that as it may, the eyes are undoubtedly the focal point of human expression, and from them and their immediate surroundings one can learn much of what is transpiring in the mind behind. With a dog surely the nose is the focal point of expression; full of sensitivity and intelligence.

While I loved Floss's brown eyes, it was the set of her nose and the delicately twitching and dilating nostrils which told me, as best I could understand, what was passing in her mind. How often when we were pottering about in the neighbourhood of the cottage would she pause with nose lifted, reading, detecting some interesting item the air brought her. She would look round at me with an enquiring lift of the nose to see what I thought about it, and I, like a blind dolt, did not know anything about it. What a fool she must have thought I was, to go blundering on regardless of the intelligence received. Up would go a couple of partridges or a rabbit would spring from the bramble, or I'd catch a glimpse of a fox streaking to cover, and Floss, almost pityingly, would come to heel and look up at me with her ears back and say, 'I told you so; why aren't you more careful?'

I tried hard to use my nose to better purpose; not that I hoped ever to emulate Floss and point a pheasant or discover that a stranger had crossed the hill during my absence, but at least I wanted my nose to make me aware of some of the interesting scents and lovely perfumes with which the countryside abounded. For, after all, we have five main senses with which to explore the world about us, and we make good use of sight, sound and touch, but taste only seems to provide us with some excuse to eat our food, and scent we hardly use at all. I cast my thoughts back to the days when I lived in London and tried to think of a single thing that my nose made me pleasantly aware of, but there was nothing but what was objectionable. Two things stuck in my mind: one was the horrible odour of grilled bones that in places rose hotly from gratings beside the pavement – I learnt these places and used to hurry by holding my breath, and the other was the foul stink which poured in a gale up the tubes and tunnels of the underground. In fact most of the powerful smells of our towns and cities and factories, and where humanity sweats and packs and crowds together, are offensive. No wonder we fail to use our fifth sense; we do not want to, and it soon atrophies. A chemist told me that he was quite insensitive to the smell of his shop. After a holiday, however, on his return to the counter, he was just as aware of the strong distinctive smell-mixture as I was, yet he told me, after three days or less he was as 'blind' to it as ever. Apparently our brains are capable of shutting off information received via the nose, given time; a sewage worker informed me that even he 'got used to it' after a while, and never noticed the stenches.

These thoughts encouraged me, for if we can shut the doors to sense of smell, there seemed no reason why we should not open them, and open them wide, and thus explore the world from a new angle. It is not possible to suggest any special technique for exercising the nose any more than it is for the eyes or ears, except that one must use them, not mechanically but with purpose. One cannot see with shut eyes, nor hear with bunged-up ears, and similarly one cannot smell with a dry nose nor with one choked with catarrh. We all know, when suffering from a cold, we cannot even smell the onions we are peeling. Dogs and most other animals maintain a very moist nose, and it would seem that it is only when the membrane within the nostrils is moist that the nose is properly sensitive to smells. I found that one of the reasons why my nose was not often in this condition was because I breathed through my mouth. By keeping my mouth shut and both inhaling and exhaling through the nose, the natural moisture carried by my breath kept my nose damp. After a sneeze, or after blowing my nose, I found I could always smell better. All this, no doubt, is obvious and elementary, but it was amusing to learn from Floss and discover things for oneself. Floss quite often sneezed, and I have a fancy most dogs can and do sneeze at will.

Keeping the nose in proper condition was, as I have said, no more than keeping the eyes open, and as with the eyes one may look and see nothing, so with the nose one may smell and perceive nothing, unless one is consciously trying to do so. Hence there were days or hours during my herb-collecting when I tried hard to contact the countryside about me by the fifth sense. Many of the herbs that I gathered were very aromatic and the richness of their fragrance, as I snapped or cut the stems or bruised the leaves, was often forced upon me. Then I would remember and spend many an interesting and delicious afternoon sampling all the scents and perfumes everywhere around me. I have already mentioned the delicate fragrance of centaury, and the sweet honey-lemon perfume of agrimony, but as the summer drew on and I found myself down in the marshland and along the banks of the Darn gathering meadowsweet and tansy, then I entered a new world.

It may have been because the air along the low levels and by the stream was particularly humid, and the essence of perfumes was more easily held in suspension, that there I detected scents more strongly; or it may have been because many of the plants that grew there were especially rich in volatile substances (perhaps for both reasons), but wherever I went, in boggy bottoms, along old, weed-clogged draining ditches, amid the lush vegetation that crowded where the Darn overflowed, I stirred and discerned rich and varied scents. Mint was always with me; I was unavoidably crushing and bruising it wherever I went cutting meadowsweet, but I was much more fond of its smell than that of wild garlic, which was so strong when I was collecting clivers. The smell of water mint and horse mint was warm and formed an almost continuous background into which or against which scents merged or stood out according to their peculiar qualities.

Meadowsweet, or the queen of the meadows as we children knew it, had a sweet fragrance as distinctive from the mint as its appearance. Only when you buried your nose right in the feathery blossom did the scent seem a little unpleasant; but is not that the way with many perfumes when taken too full? Meadowsweet did not have to be bruised or crushed before I could smell it; in fact there was very little smell attaching to stem and leaves; its fragrance was distilled from its blossoms, and it was most delicious when brought to me at a little distance by soft summer airs.

What an amazing and inexplicable thing scent really is. For me to smell the fragrance of a plant at thirty yards distance something had actually to travel from the flower to my nose, not in the form of waves or pulsations or vibrations as in the case of sound and sight, but some actual particle of itself. The scientists tell us that the molecules of substances are continually in violent motion and escaping into the air at exposed surfaces; this is particularly noticeable with liquids such as oils and alcohols. The free molecules, now presumably gaseous, travel at great speed through the molecules of air, and of course are carried by moving air, and thus reach our noses. But that is only half the story, for these tiny fagments of matter have to reach the scent cells at the upper inner end of our nostrils, when something unknown occurs, perhaps some chemical action, and then the result is telegraphed by the nerve system to the brain which interprets to us

the result – the scent of meadowsweet.

We are fearfully and wonderfully made, or, to our mortal minds, it seems so. Perhaps the ultimate truth will be far simpler. Life and its interpretation have become, or been made, exceedingly complex of recent years. No sooner have we learnt a new theory or mastered a new hypothesis than fresh revelations prove them inaccurate or untenable. Matter and movement are whisked away into mathematics, the universe is a soap bubble of stresses and strains. Yet here am I ankle-deep in marsh mud, gathering herbs, learning to contact the wonderful world about by the sense of smell. What a contradiction! I am as deeply interested as any others in the theories that attempt to explain matter and energy and light and so forth. The nearer these approach to resolving matter into mind the happier I shall be, for that will lead to simplification, and simplification is, I believe, what millions are a-seeking, particularly in the appreciation of life and beauty. For until we develop the sixth, or the sixtieth, sense, or shuffle off this mortal coil, it is only by the five main gateways that we can apprehend the significance of all created things and receive from them their blessings.

By simply listening to music I can be transported into realms of indescribable delight, fancy, beauty, movement, excitement. The technique is simple, though one does not learn to appreciate good things at once, one advances stage by stage. By simply smelling could I be transported? Without extravagance or attempting to stretch a point, indeed I could; though whither or in what terms of emotion or mind I can no more explain than I can of a glorious sunset or an Enigma variation. Scents and perfumes have a remarkable power; sometimes they exercise their influence upon us almost against our conscious thinking; but if we evoke their power their emotional effect can be great. I remember discovering the potency of the scent of sweet peas. There were certain varieties which had a most delicate fragrance, and I found, not all at once, that this scent was truly inspiring; it seemed to rush to my head and affect me like that soaring theme in *Parsifal*. It still does, though no doubt this will sound extravagant to both gardeners and music-lovers alike. I wonder. Have you never lingered over the scent of a rose, a carnation, a bunch of primroses, and been wafted away into realms of fantasy? Perhaps it would have been a world of memories conjured for you by that sweet fragrance; for although the sense of smell is probably the second oldest gateway, the most primitive distant contact with the surrounding world, few will deny that it is the most dramatic in provoking memory.

How the smell of restharrow carries me back to days of carefree childhood when my brothers and I dug a cave in a sandbank with purloined kitchen knives. And the scent of geranium to my grandfather's garden where, with blue lobelia and white alyssum, the patriotic beds surrounded the fountain. And the smell of camphor to my mother's sealskin coat, so soft, so sleek.

There were certain times in the day and night when scent hung in the air far more strongly and more widespread than at others. I could never be sure when this would occur, though it was more often in the late evening than at other times. But the 'hour of scents', as I called it, was as fickle as a maiden's smile; neither the time nor the day could be foretold. It might occur just as well in the morning, at midday or at midnight. The cause for this remarkable hour was much more than mere humidity, which condition, as I have said, probably accounted for the richness of smells near the Darn. Temperature must have had much to do with it; low temperatures certainly are not conducive to the production and dissemination of scent, neither are high temperatures necessary, though of course certain things smell more when heated. But I am thinking mainly of plants and the scent of flowers and foliage, and while both humidity and temperature must have some hand in causing the 'hour of scents', probably other atmospheric conditions do also, and not only conditions at the time, or which have preceded it, but perhaps conditions to come. The interrelation of plants, their flowers and insects, is so close that I have begun to wonder if it were not probable that scent is produced in, or prior to, conditions when there will be on the wing those very insects which the flower needs for fertilising agents. In this connection I have been interested to note that the sweet fragrance of the tobacco plant is strongest and most widely disseminated on those very twilights when the convolvulus hawk moth is on the wing, the only moth with proboscis long enough to probe the nectar at the end of the elongated corolla.

The 'hour of scents' on a still July or August night beggars description. I have known a single honeysuckle plant waft its delicious fragrance over an area of at least an acre; a veritable lake of perfume surrounded it. What the depth of the lake was I could not ascertain, much as I wanted to, for it would have been interesting to discover if the scent was radiating evenly in a hemisphere, or whether there were layers or strata of suitable air in which the fragrance so freely floated. I incline to the latter, for air does often lie in very sharply defined layers, warm and cool, humid and dry, as is easily observed when shallow mists lie on or near the ground, or one above another, and as layers of cloud so obviously do. On very still days

I have noticed smoke from bonfires and chimneys rise vertically and then, as if there were some invisible ceiling, turn abruptly at right angles and drift slowly away in a gentle, level cloud. Where there are movements of air near the ground then there is no lake, but instead streams and rivers of scent begin to trickle and pour across the meadows, through the woods and down the lane. Such streams are remarkable for keeping within very narrow bounds. It is possible to take two steps and pass right through the fragrant ribbon that floats out in the lee of a bush of sweet briar. There is a fragrance for our sweet mothers! Mine erstwhile taught me to pinch the little rough leaflets and sniff, and now I take one step backward and raise my head and sniff, and oh! my heart goes wandering up the old-fashioned garden where she dreamed dreams and I heedless played.

The scent of pines and of other coniferous trees comes drifting down the woodland path. Like a saga of heroic achievement amid fell and fjord it bears us on wings of song to Valhalla. Or perhaps it is full of the warm south, and the Mediterranean's romantic blue. But it is more even than this, more than association, more than memory; it is the scent of trees, the distilled essence of their lives, of concentrated summer sunshine, winter snows, spring rains, autumn mists, of all good things from mother earth refined.

At a few places along the banks of the Darn tansy grew, and I fancy that the seed or pieces of root were brought there years ago by the stream itself. Nowhere else in the Copsford country did I come across it, and in only one other locality, a roadside bank on the far side of the village, did I discover it. The latter was certainly a garden escape, but where the former could have come from I never discovered. Nowhere up the course of the Darn did the stream flow by or very near a garden. Possibly the folk who lived in Copsford long ago had grown it in their garden; yet somehow I do not think so, for tansy, once it gets a hold, in any soil, is well-nigh impossible to eradicate, and there was no trace of it about the cottage. There should have been a jungle of it after twenty years' neglect. I wished it had been there, not only as a herb for me to collect on my very doorstep, but because I am fond of its feathery leaves and clustering heads of golden petalless flowers, and because of its scent too. This is strong, and when the plant has been the least crushed or bruised it is overpowering, and many folk dislike it on that account, considering it coarse. But nothing reminds me so much of the Darn, its rust-coloured banks, its quiet pools, its dams of flotsam where root and branch hold in check leaves and twigs and rubbish till the next flood, and of water voles which swim and dive in the vasty deeps or shoot the prattling cataracts.

Being confined to a few clumps along the brook, tansy was not a large harvest, and because it was un-thinned and crowded about with dense herbage, it grew tall and thin and reedy with all its lower leaves brown and shrivelled. About fifty pounds fresh was all I gathered, but I intended to supplement this by gathering from that roadside beyond the village. Alas, when I reached it someone had forestalled me. No, not another Green Man, but the roadman; he had been trimming the banks, and there lay all my tansy cut, black, withered and useless after a week's exposure to sun and rain. It was a grievous discovery, and was not to be the only occasion when I was forestalled in this manner.

Meadowsweet and tansy have had many uses, both culinary and medicinal. Each has been a remedy for children's ailments, and the former, as its old name mead sweet suggests, was used, and I believe still is, in the making of mild beverages. Culpeper said that 'it takes away the fits of the quartan agues, and that it maketh a merry heart, for which some use the flowers and some use leaves'.

About this time the herb harvest at Copsford was at its peak; not a room, except my bedroom, but was crammed with drying plants. Even the desolate scullery was pressed into service, and a dozen strings were run from wall to wall and were immediately hung with curtain after curtain of meadowsweet and tansy. It was an astonishing sight. The August weather had been fairly kind and herbs had dried fast enough for me to be able continuously, almost daily, to replace, in one room or another, dried herb with fresh. The dry was bagged up at once and the little storeroom was a satisfying sight with its many bulging and heavy sacks. I was pleased with my successful harvesting, and though I had no idea what quantity of dried herb I now had, because my scales would not record over a quarter, the size and number of sacks did look good. I was so thrilled with it all that at last I dared venture to ask the music mistress to come over and inspect, and, on the pretext of helping me to gather meadowsweet, she came.

I had much to do that morning, sweeping the worst of the litter from the floors, soothing Floss who had caught the excitement either from my unusual exertions or the absurd snatches of song I uttered, discovering if there was anything at all to eat for tea or anything clean to put it on, pondering on the impropriety of asking her to have tea in my bedroom, which was the only place where one could sit down in a chair (one chair) and not have insects fall from drying herbs on to one's bread and butter, and the hundred other problems which beset a worried bachelor trying to prepare an impossible, derelict cottage to receive an important personage. For, after all, I had got used to the place. I scarcely saw the broken windows, bare and blistered woodwork, clumsily patched floor, ugly stark brick, cavernous sooty fireplace and makeshift everything. All I now saw in Copsford was a place to dry and store herbs, a place where Floss and I could sleep and eat, where we could get moderate shelter during unpleasant weather. But that morning, as I swept the dust and rubbish out of the front door, the scales of familiarity fell from my eyes and I saw the place as I had first seen it, and I heartily wished I had never asked her to come and see it.

But I need not have worried. She came and inspected Copsford as though it were the palace of industry. She inhaled the sweet mixture of many herbs as though it were a rose in her garden.

'It does smell good,' she said.

She eyed the array of sacks in the storeroom with keen approval. She peeped into my bedroom-cum-office-cum-sitting-room, and said that it looked light and quite comfortable, and never seemed to notice the stain in the comer of the ceiling and the huge discoloured patch on my new sunshine wallpaper where the roof had let in recent showers.

We collected great bundles of meadowsweet from the paradise of the marsh, and on return to the cottage, while I removed and folded the stiff dry herb and crammed it into sacks, she was pleased to fill the spaces with the fresh herb we had just gathered.

'What about some tea?' I ventured, with my heart in my mouth.

'Lovely; let's picnic out on the hill.'

Well, could anything have been simpler? Why hadn't I thought of that? We men are clumsy fools sometimes. There was the afternoon sun, the blue sky, the warm dry grass; surely no tea room was better appointed. And she had brought a cake of her own making to add to my bread and butter.

Floss behaved like a lady-in-waiting. She was a one-man dog, but that made no difference to her delight in the presence of a visitor, a mistress she would adore. As near as nothing I said as much, and only just bit my tongue in time. Floss took bread and butter with dainty grace, but when she discovered the cake she begged unashamed.

After tea she did a ballet dance, running round and round us where we sat, and leaping and twisting in the air, and pouncing, now and again pausing to approach and nuzzle one of us, the silky tassel of her nonexistent tail oscillating with pleasure at our praise. How dogs do restore the balance in delicate situations!

Our visitor had gone. After a tactful chat with the farmer's wife she had gone. With milk and water I walked slowly back to Copsford. Floss met me, quiet and subdued, and we sat on the bed a long time looking at nothing.

Sometimes at the height of a summer day, when the sun is warm and the bees hum and all seems set for an endless season, suddenly for some slight thing, almost unconsciously discerned, the end is determined, the first breath of autumn is drawn in the midst of summer. I have known the same thing in the depth of winter, a twitter of birdsong, hazel catkins shaking loose their gold dust, perhaps the scent of mimosa or just a patch of blue sky, and one hears the first rustle of spring's awakening. Winter is doomed.

As I sat with Floss's head in my lap, gazing away into the gathering dusk of a perfect summer day, was I aware that something was inexorably ending? Could the sign have been that discoloured patch above my head? And if I was aware, did I know then that wherever there is an end there is also a beginning?

EYEBRIGHT

MY CHOICE OF COPSFORD for a herb centre was more fortunate than I ever imagined. Although the surrounding country was almost exclusively woodland and rough, uncultivated pasture, with, of course, the Darn and marshland, the variety of herbs which grew there in sufficient quantity to be worth gathering was quite remarkable. When I first came I had thought that three, or at the most four, harvests would have been all that the countryside could provide, and as much as I could manage. Yet by August I had bags of clivers, foxglove, centaury, agrimony, meadowsweet and tansy, and far more of some of them than I had thought that I, single-handed, could possibly have collected. Another noteworthy advantage had been the fact that these herbs which my countryside provided had followed one another without break from May to September. The seasons for their harvesting had been continuous, they had overlapped; sometimes I was gathering three different plants at the same time, but there had been no gaps. There had never been a day, apart from wet weather, when I could not go out and gather something.

Eyebright was a most unexpected little harvest. I scarcely remembered ever seeing the plant before, and only came across it by accident when exploring a small heathy strip of land on the other side of the Darn. It is an inconspicuous little herb and yet with a most charming habit. It is like a tiny, bushy shrub, never more than a few inches high, but so branched and ramified as to appear a ball. Its leaves are stemless, small and snipped round the edges, in pairs, and the flowers are small too, but very sweet, white with purple and yellow markings. What a magnificent garden shrub it would make were it but magnified a dozen times.

It had a very curious smell, most noticeable when drying, and I never could quite bring myself to like it. There was something oily and a little frowsty about it. Yet, as its name suggests, it was greatly esteemed by the herbalists. Old Culpeper says, 'If the herb was but as much used as it is neglected, it would half spoil the spectacle makers' trade; and a man would think that reason should teach people to prefer the preservation of their natural before artificial spectacles.' We cannot but be charmed and somewhat amused at such confidence and quaint turn of phrase. I know not to what use the eyebright was put that I collected. Perhaps it went to 'strengthen the weak brain or memory', and I have a quiet hope that as 'Arnoldus de Villa Nova saith, it hath restored sight to them that have been blind a long time'.

Eyebright seems to prefer a heathy type of country with perhaps a sandy or stony soil. I have noticed it since on banks and in woodland clearings or following the woodcutter, on commons, and in old meadows, where birch and gorse and broom grow. Heathery moor crowds it out as it does most other plants; nevertheless, eyebright enjoys elevation, and most of my recollections of it are coupled with breezy open spaces.

What a relief it is to throw oneself down on one's back, where the grass is crisp and dry and, with arms outspread, relax, and gaze into the blue depths of the sky! Lying there one can dream while wide awake. I glide into a new world where everything is upside down. I stare into a deep sea, a mighty ocean, bottomless, if any ocean were so. Am I floating on its surface, or what is this that grips my back so firmly that I shall not sink into its depths? I would like to plunge, then I would pass beyond the waving tops of the inverted silver birches, down, down, to those false bottoms of pearly rippling light where no foot can ever tread. It is a strange ocean, for in its depths there are islands, shores and continents which pass and dissolve before my eyes.

I wake with a start, only to discover that now I am lying on the floor of the ocean, looking up through its translucent depths to the faraway surface. The clouds are now spindrift flying before the wind. Sometimes that surface is scarcely ruffled and the foam is tinted like mother-of-pearl, in hues of pink and green and silvery sheen; sometimes it is heavily furrowed, and full of storm. Then there are the great ships, with crowded sail, that set steady course to the northeast, their black bottoms passing overhead, the shadows of their hulls gliding across the ocean floor.

With a jolt I wake again and, sitting up, watch those cloud shadows sliding sinuously over rolling wood and undulating pastures. Close to the heathy knoll they race by with the speed of a homing pigeon, but over beyond the cottage they glide so slowly that by walking one imagines one could keep pace with them. Few things are as lovely as cloud-play across the countryside. Colours blaze out and are extinguished in a miraculous manner. There are the birches beyond the osier bed alight and brilliant, shimmering, then, like a hand drawing a veil, they grow dark, almost sombre by contrast with the bordering meadows, which now glow like emeralds; a wheatfield suddenly turns from rust to gold, then a wood takes fire, green fire with darting yellow flames, where some chestnut and beech think of autumn. A group of pines springs into bold relief, coppery columns with mossy canopies, only in the twinkling of an eye to retreat again, dark, cold and sullen.

Once in October, from the same vantage ground, I watched a group of young aspens. They had escaped from the boundaries of a wood and spread out into an old rough-and-tumble, never-mown meadow, forming a little graded plantation of their own. You know how the leaves of aspens tremble; well, these were trembling in a chilly autumn breeze, but they were all a dear golden yellow. Suddenly a beam of sunshine swept across the meadow like a fingering searchlight and pointed with dramatic intensity at those trembling aspens. Oh my heart! No one can describe such tremulous glory. Gold, words, poetry are but dross beside such beauty. Like a grand chord of music, my eyes saw the wonder. The light passed, the music died away, the aspen leaves fluttered dully in the shadow. The vision faded. A few days later, when there was more sunshine, I went hoping to see the wonder repeated, but every leaf had fallen, the chord was never to be struck again. Many a time while at Copsford, and since, I have blundered accidentally into some untrodden dell or little clearing and found beauty there enshrined that, but for the merest chance, none would ever have beheld. I think of the countless other nooks and glades, flowers and colours, scents and sounds, that no one ever perceives, and I am deeply moved by that prodigality which scatters beauty with so lavish a hand everywhere around us.

The play of wind across long grass was another thing which held me idling, but enchanted, among the eyebright. The wind is taken so much for granted except when damaging or dangerous, that we scarcely ever notice the fascinating things this invisible conjurer can do. When I lived in London I cannot recollect a single instance in which I took notice with pleasure of what the wind was doing. I remember, during that last winter, that I was cold when a northeaster blew down my miserable street and pierced my threadbare overcoat. I remember watching the smoke roll sombrely away from the four black Satanic chimneys of the power station, and was uncomfortably impressed on January evenings when the dull fire of sunset was trapped among their belching columns; and although the wind blew chilly off the cold grey Thames and whistled in the iron rigging of the bridge which was my vantage ground, I thought nothing of it except as another unpleasant element in this dramatic setting of enslaved humanity. The freedom that I won by living in that lonely cottage brought me into touch with real nature in a way that I had never understood to be possible. 'Into touch' is a poor, worn-out phrase, yet I find great difficulty in expressing in comprehensive terms exactly what I mean. It was closer contact than touch, it was almost union. All about me seemed to have an importance for me, they entered into my life and I into theirs. The birds, animals, trees, plants, insects, all meant or brought something to my life. I felt their presence. Gradually I became vividly aware of sound and music, form and colour, and not only of living things but of the elemental things which make their world our world. I became, as I have said, more sensitive to light, my sense of smell brought me new contacts, movement was language.

I found delight in simple things which before I neither noticed nor heeded Wind-play over unmown grass fascinated me. From a little deviation one can look down upon a meadow, or, if the field slopes upwards, one can watch from below. Every puff and gust of wind, every whirl and eddy as it plays across the field is recorded among the tall grasses. They bend and sway, recover and nod again, and, every time they move, the light glances from their bent and glossy stems and leaves, and a silvery patch is born and moves and glides, and hurries away downwind. I call them my wind sheep. They come through the hedge at the lower end. I never see them coming, but I see the hedge shaking and I know that they are there. See, some are already in the meadow, just a few moving slowly up the slope. Now others have joined them, and look, a whole lot more have come through the hedge, farther along. There they go, scores, no hundreds of them. Some are running fast, they are swarming up the hill in strings and flocks and herds. How silvery-white their backs glisten in the sun, how patiently and persistently they hurry on! Never one dare linger or stray. Up the long slope they unceasingly trek as if all the sheep of the veldt were on the move. At last they reach the other hedge, and leaping from the waving grasses, they vanish. But regardless of the fate of their leaders, the cavalcade presses continuously onward, until at length the old sheepdog tires and sleeps in his southwest kennel, then the last of the wind sheep lie down in the meadows and the swaying grasses are still.

I spent lazy hours on my little heath. They were hot September days, and after a dip in the shadowed brook I would scramble up through the bracken and find a grassy nook in the gorse bushes where I could sun and watch and listen. There was a continuous snapping and popping as the dried gorse pods burst open and flung their seeds away. I never saw one split; it always seemed that it was the pod behind me, or beside me, or above my head, and never the ones I was looking at that burst. I could hear the seeds fall. Sometimes they fell on my face as I watched the clouds. Nearby was a linnet's nest; the young had long since flown, but there was still one egg left embedded in the bottom of it. I was sorry to be short of one linnet, for they are charming birds, their soft musical trill is the theme song of the furze; and what a gay fellow the cock is with his crimson crown, pink breast and chestnut mantle, when seen really close up. There is very little bird music in late summer, but now and again I heard the curious 'twarr-twarr' note of bullfinches. To me it was just like the noise we children used to make holding a piece of elastic in our mouth and twanging it with one hand as we stretched it tight with the other. A family of long-tailed tits frequently flitted through the bushes, but only when very dose could I detect their high-pitched tiny voices. It astonished me, however, that they could make their way so easily, so speedily, yet quite unhurt, among the tangled thorns and cruel spikes. I have never seen a bird impaled on gorse.

Where rabbits had made a great scratching of loose sandy soil, birds were continuously coming to dust bath. Pheasants and partridges made a big to-do; they grovelled in it, scratching and fluttering and then standing and rustling their feathers and shaking their wings till they were enveloped in clouds of dust. After these companions of the bath had finished their revellings, the pheasants striding in lordly manner to go down to the marsh, and the partridges ducking and 'tcheking' to wander to some old fallow, smaller birds would take their turn. They almost burrowed in the sandy dust, scrabbling along like little legless mice; then they would sit in a shallow hollow of their own making and spread their wings and raise and separate their feathers and sun, just as I was doing. I must say, though, that I never tried the dry dust-bath. One could scarcely explain such behaviour by declaring that one was considering the birds. I have not yet noticed birds dust-bathing in winter, and whether this is because there is little dust then, or because their skin and feathers do not require it, or simply because I am unobservant, I cannot say. But birds will water-bathe at all seasons of the year, in the heat of August, during pouring rain, even when there is snow and frost in January and February. They are all-the-year-rounders, and such enthusiasts, casting up showers of spray, and coming back again and again for more. And the enthusiasm is infectious; others crowd round, queuing up about the edge of the puddle to await their turn, and getting a free shower in the meantime.

On account of the somewhat heathy nature of the knoll, with its dry, rather sandy soil, plants grew there which I did not commonly find elsewhere. Along with the gorse there was much broom, and while the gorse flowers all the year – they say it is kissing-time when the gorse is in flower – the broom has a very brief flowering season. But what a brave show it makes. Surely no other wild shrub of ours is quite so gay. I love its dense green slender stems beset with numberless blossoms, which all seem to come out together. Where the gorse is orange, the broom is lemon; while the gorse has a glorious fragrance, broom has nothing; the gorse is stiff and prickly, the broom soft and pliant. One seems the counterpart of the other, yet they are not often growing in close company. After the butterfly blooms have withered, broom looks a little ragged and untidy, but the grey-green pods soon lengthen and later turn black, and they too split suddenly and with a sharp twist both halves of the pod spring asunder and flick the flat glossy seeds to the heather. Not much heather in my case, in the Copsford country, but just enough perhaps to foreshadow the Gates of Eden, where I caught my first glimpse of the purple-clad hills of Scotland, and carved a name on a tree where none but I could find it.

Ling, heath, broom, furze, that is what I sometimes think Shakespeare did write. When I was sitting there among the gorse I knew that if ever Gonzalo had sat in quiet serene on sunny common with the sea far away a silvery streak, then indeed, when it roared and raged and threatened to engulf him in watery grave, he would cry from his heart 'Ling, heath, broom, furze, anything'. Only in the cloistered classroom does 'long heath, brown furze' sound more sweetly in the scholar's ear.

But what are we coming to if a mere Green Man comments on Shakespearean text? Suffice it to say that when I saw the wild green-grey sea bursting over the fo'c'sle, frothing in the scuppers, bouncing in mad spray over the bridge, when I saw the dirty horizon heaving deliriously up and down, and when my tight-clamped ears heard the tingling whisper of the sinister doings of submarine craft, then was I sick for home, then would my heart cry for eyebright, heartsease, wood sage, ragwort, anything. Anything that was dry and warm and still.

YARROW

About Copsford Cottage there was an enclosure which in the past might have been a well-cultivated garden. From what old John Guy had said it had certainly been in use in his day, some forty years before, and naturally I had visions of restoring it, or at least of cultivating some of it. There was a narrow strip across the front between the tumbledown fence and the cottage; this widened on either side, and at the back there was quite a piece of some seven or eight rods. But the hedges on either side were fifteen feet high, and suckers, nettles and brambles encroached many yards. Also there were dense tangles in the centre, and about the old well, and beyond there was the tall, shady, overgrown shaw. I could see I could do nothing with the back, at least until I had the tools for the job, but the front and the south side were quite clear except for trampled grass, and here I thought I might begin my husbandry. I had ideas of growing vegetables, of perhaps growing more valuable herbs than those I collected wild, and vaguely of beautifying the cottage by covering up some of that harsh, naked brick.

So I borrowed a spade from the farmer. He was more tickled than puzzled this time.

'You be goin' to dig the garden then?' he queried with a twinkle, scraping the cow muck from his boots the meanwhile on the very spade he was going to lend me.

'Slow job an' all,' he commented, handing me both spade and dung.

'But nothin' like startin' early. I'll look in on ye one day and see as 'ow ye be gettin' on.'

I thanked him and strode off, and I must say that I felt a bit of a fool. I don't know why. It might have been that remark of his about starting early, and I was sure that, as I walked away, he and his good wife were looking out of the kitchen window and having a good laugh.

It was no use attempting anything of a garden at the cottage until I had a fence to keep out the farmer's bullocks and horses, or later in the year, his keep sheep. So I did my best to mend or replace some of the old fence which was my front boundary. It was the sort of fence which is made up of triangular bars fitting into vertical slots in the posts. The old oak posts were still there, after all those years, but many of them were much awry from the constant rubbing and nudging of cattle. They were so firm in the hard, dry ground that I could not possibly pull them into the perpendicular. Hence my improvised bars had to fit and strain and slope in a very Heath Robinson manner. But a rough fence they did make and I thought it would suffice.

I began to dig. Began is not the right word – I tried to dig. I took the spade and attempted to hew off the rough grass. In theory this was very simple and very correct. After taking off a neat heap of sods I would burn them, then I would set to work to do the real digging. How vainly does man propose! The grass which had had its own way for a couple of decades refused stubbornly to budge; its coarse, tufted roots and stems were like iron wire. And the spade (damn it) – if ever I swore I did then – the spade was as blunt as hell, with an edge like the back of a comb. I jabbed, I slashed, I sliced, I stubbed my wrists and nearly put out my right thumb. In three days, in between my harvesting of yarrow, I had but cleared as many square yards. Floss had never witnessed such behaviour. She sat, she lay at a safe distance, and watched, I believe, with quiet amusement. When I haggled off a particularly wiry bit she would seize upon it, toss it in the air with merry sport, pretend not to see where it fell, and then suddenly pounce upon it when it was not looking and worry it, as she would a rat. Then she would drop it and come back to see more sparks fly.

At the end of the fourth day there was a hideous, bald, uneven patch under one window. The time had come to dig. But, ye gods, could I get the spade into that unyielding glebe? Not only had the ground been sunbaked under the cottage wall, but it had been the stamping ground of many cloven hoofs for many years. And how cloven hoofs can ram! The farmer told me that if you want some ground beaten hard nothing can beat sheep at the job; and I have since been told that a pin rammer is far more effective than the usual large club-footed affair. Whatever the truth of this, the ground about Copsford was like concrete. I could do no more than flake off chips, the spade leaving a hard, glassy sear wherever I did so. It sounds absurd, but it just could not be dug. A pickaxe would have been little better, and I remember in my disgust that I thought the only tool which could have made any real impression would have been one of those pneumatic drills that made such a hateful din in the streets of London. I almost wished I had had one to wreak my vengeance on that garden-not-to-be, but it would have been cutting off my nose to spite my face.

Two nights later I woke suddenly with Floss barking furiously within the bedroom. I lit the candle. She was in a terrible rage; her mane stood on end in a great ruff, and all down her spine her hair stood up in a stiff ridge. I was startled; since the rat war she had never behaved like this. Surely the rats were not returning. In a flash I remembered an old fellow telling me that rats changed their quarters once a year, when, led by a gigantic brute called the king rat, they trekked from farm to farm or village to village, in a great procession, and any who dared hinder or check their progress might be attacked as desperately as by a pack of wolves. I shuddered; suppose they were going to inhabit Copsford in a mighty army. Suddenly Floss stopped her strident barking and we listened, taut and silent. It was a quiet moonless September night, and at first, after Floss's shrill barking, I could hear nothing. Then I was aware of a low rumbling or thudding, a pause, and then the thudding repeated. Floss was about to bark again but I hushed her with silent threats, and reached for the little gun. But security had led to neglect, and it was unloaded and the elastic half perished. There was more rumbling and I felt my hair creep. Then without the slightest warning there was a sharp crack. In the stillness of the night it was like a pistol shot and it was too much for Floss, who raced round the room like a mad thing, barking to wake the dead. I flung the bedroom door open so that she could descend the stairs and work off some of her rage and noise in the lower regions. She went down like a cataract. For myself, although that crack had well-nigh stopped my heart, I was easier in mind. No legion of rats could have caused that, and I guessed at once what was happening. I wedged the window open and leaned out: sure enough, after a few seconds of accommodating my eyes to darkness, I distinguished bulky forms crowded about the cottage. Only cattle – but sometimes one is mighty thankful for an anticlimax. Floss, of course, must have known it was the farm animals from the beginning, but she knew also they were trespassing. Perhaps, before I woke, they had already broken my improvised fence and roused Floss, but there they certainly were, in my garden, cows, bullocks, calves and no doubt the old bull as well, pin-ramming my garden-not-to-be.

Relief gave way to anger. All my pent-up fury from wrestling with that stubborn soil was let loose. The brutes! They were the cause of my fruitless labours, they were breaking down my fence even now, they had startled the breath out of me. I fumbled downstairs and, egging Floss on with shouts of encouragement, I jerked the front door open and let the whirlwind out. There was a stampede, grunts and bellowings and stamping feet; some went through what was left of the fence with cracks and groans, some went round the back of the house with Floss yelping behind them. She had them round on the other side of the house in a twinkling and within a few seconds the whole mob were careering down the hill chivied by man and dog. It would have been an amazing spectacle could anyone but have witnessed it, for I found on returning to the cottage that in my alarm and indignation I had leapt from the bed and rushed to the attack without donning a single garment.

The morning brought a sad spectacle. If anything more had been wanting completely to discourage my labours for a cottage garden, this was it. My fence was a wreck, a ruin of bars broken, bars crushed, bars pushed out of sockets and strewn about the place, and cowpats everywhere. The bull and his families had a right of way around Copsford and evidently were determined to keep it open. I was beaten and gave up the idea of cottage gardening. The wilderness returned to its own, and never again would anyone attempt cultivation about those grim walls till they tumbled into ruin. So I mused as I cleared up the mess and wondered incidentally how my naked feet could have missed so much.

Yarrow took me to the haunts of men. It was not to be found in woods and spinneys, it was rarely in meadow or rough pasture. It grew in cultivated ground, in fallow along newly made roadsides and banks, wherever soil was turned or broken. So I deserted my wild, unkempt countryside and went back to the highway and the farm. And I was late for this harvest, for time and again farmer and roadman forestalled me. I would note on my wanderings a fine crop of weeds along the embankment of a new by-pass. There was yarrow standing up thick and strong, its ferny, fine-cut foliage and its masses of white, sometimes pinkish flowers, making to my eyes a fine and welcome harvest. This I would determine to come and collect the next fine morning, and a few days later I would be there with my borrowed bicycle. But it was the tansy disaster all over again; the yarrow was felled or burned, or altogether had disappeared. It did not happen once but several times; it almost seemed as if I was the Council Surveyor who, having located a tiresome crop of weeds, immediately sent someone to clear them away. That someone, it appeared, had a spite against all Green Men, me in particular; there was the hidden hand of persecution. I grew furtive, and if I noticed any yarrow, pretended not to see it, but took great pains to be interested in something else.

On the farm lands it was much the same. I would locate a good crop of yarrow on a field of half-cleared brassica, but by the time I was able to see about it the plough had been put in, and all I could see of my yarrow was some of its roots and a few muddied flowers peeping from beneath the furrows. I once arrived when a friendly farmer was in the very act of ploughing some fallow. Hastily gathering what yarrow still remained, I then sat down and watched him. Although I know nothing at all about the art, I find ploughing extremely fascinating – with a team of horses, that is. Tractor ploughing loses half its appeal. The horses appear so willing; to me it always seems they like this work, they put such zest into it. The

magnificent action of their strong limbs, their rhythmic nod, free-flowing
manes and tails, their understanding of the work and ready response to the
ploughman, all appeal to me tremendously. To which is added the perfect
action of the ploughshare and the delightful clean, curving fold of the brown
soil, peeling away from polished steel like the bow wave of a battleship.
I talked to the farmer about it when he next came to rest; but while I
could see he loved ploughing as much as I loved skating, he was somewhat
inarticulate, and perhaps he thought I was not altogether sincere, or that I
was making too light of his task. Anyhow, unexpectedly he suggested that
I should take his place. Of course I protested that I had never touched a
plough or turned a furrow in my life, and that I should only make a mess
of his perfect work. But he would take no excuse, and put my hand to the
plough I must. The horses, he said, would manage without my interference,
and I must say I was grateful to those two fine beasts.

Away we went. How shall I describe my experience?

Those to whom ploughing is regular work may smile, those who
would never dream of such a task might jeer, for, after all, what is there in
ploughing anyway to make a song about? Nevertheless those few hectic
minutes were an unforgettable experience and one that I would not have
missed for a hundred bags of yarrow. I was acutely conscious of the power
of those horses. I felt they would pull me away over the horizon. I had
control over that power and had to direct it, transform it, lead it into
the ploughshare. The plough had to be guided, not only in a straight line
parallel with the last furrow but also in depth. Of course the horses went
away dead straight up the previous furrow, so there was no risk of my
careering in a mad course all over the field, but there was nothing to stop
me swerving enough to break a snake's back. A plough looks a rough-and-
ready, cumbrous thing, just sort of knocked together for a dirty old clumsy
job, yet really it is the most perfect implement, the product of centuries
of laborious endeavour, that does exactly the work that is required of it.
Exactly, that is, in the hands of the skilled ploughman. A chisel in the
hands of a craftsman can shape a lily, in the hands of a fool it will make
matchwood. A plough in the hands of an expert will carve a perfect line, an

even width, a steady depth; in the hands of a novice it might do anything. Yes, indeed, sometimes I was so near the edge, or so shallow, or both, that the horses fairly stumbled forward at the sudden unexpected reduction of their load, and the plough was almost torn out of my hands as I staggered after it, struggling to get it under control. Again, I swerved so wide or drove it so deep that the ploughshare seemed to sink into the earth, and then, like giants, the horses strove to overcome the tremendous load I had thrust upon them. They must have known there was a fool behind; but no matter what idiotic mistakes I made – and I must have made them all – they took no heed, they knew their work, they pulled straight on.

It was exhilarating and exhausting, exacting and fascinating, all at the same moment, but even as I stumbled along, straining every muscle, sweating and slipping, grasping those handles as though I were steering a ship in a heavy sea, I was conscious of elation and of triumph. I was ploughing my lone furrow.

I came back at length to the starting-point, and the farmer halted the team. I released the handles as one who lets fall the handles of a shocking coil when the almost unbearable electromotive force is switched off. I staggered like a drunken man, like a sailor ashore from heaving decks. I tried to walk, and the ground before my feet undulated in an extraordinary wave-like manner as if every yard in front of me was about to heel over before an invisible ploughshare. Except in extreme giddiness I had never experienced such a sensation. Years ago someone had taught us lads a trick, not one perhaps to be recommended, of setting a short stick in the ground, then bending to it with our heads on our hands and walking round it in this position eight or ten times, after which we were to stand up and walk a short distance. The effect was amazing. Not only did the world seem to gyrate, but it did so, not in a horizontal plane, but oblique. One struggled to stand upright on such a ridiculously sloping playground and almost invariably fell against it. I was shocked to see the eyes of some of the boys when performing this feat; they looked quite insane. I suppose when doing it I looked the same, because for a few seconds I felt the world had gone mad.

I have since wondered if I had the same wild look in my eyes when ended my furrow. Perhaps the farmer had played this trick on me for that very purpose. But of course I was not giddy, I was partially hypnotised. I had kept my eyes so fixedly concentrated upon the line of the rolling furrow, and brought into play every nerve and muscle in my body to maintain it, that although the effort only lasted three or four minutes, my brain persisted in interpreting whatever my eyes saw just as it had been doing with such fierce intensity during the ploughing. It was strange to reflect that while my eyes were for certain seeing the solid ground, yet it appeared to be rolling. How could this be? Was it a little illustration of what we hear and see, because we have heard and seen it habitually, being false?

It is interesting that things we do with enthusiastic concentration enter into our ordinary lives in a peculiar way. I remember when my brother and I learnt, during a Christmas holiday, to play chess. We took it up with such zest that, as schoolboys say, we 'properly got it on the brain'. I often felt I was a chess piece and had critical moves to make, and then the actions of others had peculiar significance. When someone passed me the bread and butter it was P to K4 which my brother snatched *en passant*. A man running up the pavement and suddenly crossing the road was obviously a knight's move and I must beware. I castled when I changed places with the boy in the desk beside me, and I trembled before the onslaught of a bishop as the master strode across the classroom.

The farmer was asking me if I liked ploughing. It was my turn to be inarticulate. 'I-I like – I think it's – it's work – grand work,' was all I could stammer. He smiled pleasantly and looked up the serpentine furrow that was my work. 'A blind man'd be pleased to see it,' he said. Then starting up the team, away he went, and a clean, even brown fold overlay my scalloping. I was grateful to him and his fine animals. Ploughing is more than a sentimental picture of diagonal lines with man and horses under a high sky. It is an art, an art that calls for strength and skill, experience and endurance, a fine eye and a quiet temper. And that says nothing of hand and voice that shall control living horse power, and the geometrician's mind that shall plan parallel ups and downs at even intervals across fields of every imaginable shape.

Yarrow brought me into contact with more folk than all the other herbs put together. I might have said into collision, for strangely enough, wherever I collected it, something seemed to go against the grain. I met another farmer whose land I very rarely crossed and he was furious to find me 'trespassin'. He wanted to know whether I'd got a 'right to be wanderin' all over these 'ere fields a-pickin' flowers'. Attempting to explain that I was gathering a herb which was a common weed among his swedes did not improve matters.

'That ain't nothin',' he snarled, throwing down the stick of yarrow that I offered him. 'That's what they call "yah". Ain't no good to nobody.'

Feeling my way through this cloud of negatives, I hesitated to suggest that in that case he might be grateful for my weeding it out; I felt he would consider that impertinence. So I said I was sorry if I had pulled out some weeds that he wanted.

'I don't want the stuff,' he bawled. 'And I don't want you a-trouchin' round after it neither.'

Well, dogs and mangers, that was that! So I apologised again and trusted that he would raise no objection to my taking away the few pieces of 'yah' that were already pulled. But he stamped off with neither refusal nor permission, only muttering inaudibly about 'yah'. I was tempted to add 'boo'.

Of course he had every right to turn me off, and I did not take umbrage, for I knew what a curse a certain type of person could be, taking every liberty on another's property. But there are, unfortunately, undesirable types of farmers also, knowing only their own rights, caring nothing for the feelings, labours and loves of others. If I had gone to his house direct for permission to gather yarrow on his land I knew I should have got the direct refusal. Seeing that I could do no harm, but actually good in pulling up his yarrow, it seemed well to do it without permission. No doubt that was very wrong of me; you cannot do good for people against their will – or can you? Perhaps not if the doer also benefits, though I suppose we all do good to our own ultimate good. But this was too involved to follow through, and no doubt I was applying false arguments to soothe my bruise.

So I gathered my yarrow elsewhere and made friends elsewhere. The crops were not large. The farmers were few and I was too late for the yarrow. By the end of September Copsford was almost empty and seemed as bare as the day when we take down Christmas decorations. I did not like it. I felt at a loss. The spectre of unemployment became daily grimmer as my strings and shelves emptied, and the bare, grimy walls came into view. What harvest of herbs would there be for me to collect during autumn and winter? There was nothing in the way of fresh herbs except sweet chestnut leaves; otherwise there were only roots, and I knew I would never take roots, however desperate my plight. Of course, I had planned when I first took Copsford to collect herbs in the spring and summer and write in the autumn and winter. But the harvesting had gone with such a swing, I had been so enormously happy, never finding the fine days long enough to do all that I wanted to do, that I found myself unable to face inaction. I had inverted the little French proverb *la cigale et la fourmi* ('the grasshopper and the ant'), and I, who had worked all the summer, now found that I was unable to sing when work was over and singing was urgent.

A spell of heavy wet weather during the first few days of autumn brought this very forcibly home to me. Everything was left desolate, every shelf barren. There was not a stick or string of any herb hung to dry anywhere in the cottage. I wandered about disconsolate; only in the storeroom, where many bulging bags lay piled on top of one another, could I pause and satisfy my soul with the sight of the harvest gathered in. Even this simple satisfaction was to receive a rude jolt. I decided to pass some of my time sewing up the sacks of dry herb preparatory to their dispatch on rail. So one miserable morning, after nearly ten days of almost continuous rain, I went into the storeroom with raffia needle and ball of thin string and prepared to sew up the bags of clivers. Opening a sack's mouth, I had the cruellest disappointment of many a long year, even including the days of rejected manuscripts – the clivers were mouldy!

I stared at it, unable to believe my eyes; my heart sank, my brain throbbed, my lips became hot and dry. Was this the end of all my labours? For although I knew next to nothing about herbs and their uses, I knew enough to know that mouldy herbs were worse than useless, as worthless as mouldy bread, as lifeless as mildewed seed, possibly as dangerous as tainted food. I wilted, I leaned against the wall too sick to move. I felt like an artist who discovers a malicious rent right across his completed canvas, or an author whose MS book has been carelessly destroyed on a bonfire in an over-zealous tidying-up. I gazed blankly at all those sacks, those sacks that had been my joy and pride. I almost hated them, lounging there so big and bulgy, distended, distorted, coarse, hiding God-knew-what iniquity within.

Slowly, as so often happens, bitter disappointment changed to fury. I grabbed at my bag of clivers, my very first bag, and tore out the top hanks of herb to discover if that damned blight penetrated the entire sack. As I disturbed it, the mould, which had developed in delicate lines along the edges of those four-sided stems, released its tiny spores in frowsty clouds of fine dust. It got in my nose and throat till coughing and sneezing made me weep as I clawed it out and flung it from the room. At first it seemed the whole sack was doomed, but then quite suddenly the rot stopped, and about halfway down the sack, the clivers came out as perfect as I had packed it. This was heartening. Perhaps the disaster was not so serious as it had at first appeared. Why had it mildewed only halfway down the sack? I remembered its position in the storeroom; it had been the first sack, up close to the window, the lower half of the sack had been well below the windowsill. The top half had been exposed to a draught of outside air coming in through a long narrow gap between the frame and the brickwork. That was it. All the time the weather was dry the draught could do no harm, but as soon as it changed then the dry herb absorbed moisture like a sponge and as soon as that happened it moulded. An immediate and thorough inspection disclosed one other bag of clivers slightly affected, and one bag of agrimony about one-third useless. The rest, thank heaven, were untouched. It does not sound a very great loss, and I was immensely relieved, to say the least, to be let off so lightly; nevertheless, about half a hundredweight of dried herb had to be thrown away, and half a hundredweight of dried herb meant anything up to two hundred pounds of fresh herb collected in the first instance, and it was this wasted effort which upset me rather than any thought of pecuniary loss.

But I had learnt my lesson. Dried, bagged herbs cannot be stored in any room where they will be subject to the vagaries of the weather. Ventilation and a steady gentle temperature are essential. Quick disposal is better. So at once I set about the business of selling them, and in the meantime I bought a little paraffin-oil stove which I left alight day and night in the storeroom. Many times afterwards I had nightmare fancies of what might have happened had I not gone up that morning with needle and string to sew up the sacks; and every time this horror visited me I would rush up to the storeroom to see if the stove were still alight. It burnt about a pint a day, and this meant, including the oil for the primus, about two gallons a week; and not only would this make a big hole in my small pocket, but it was an irksome job lugging paraffin by the two or three gallons from the village to the farm, over the field, across the Darn, and up the hill to the cottage. What with daily water and milk, posting and food-purchasing, oil and methylated, and my visits to the music mistress, I found that I was spending more than half my time travelling to and fro. How I managed it I find difficult to imagine. Today one journey from the village to Copsford and back in wet and heavy weather would be more than enough. Yet at that time I often did three and occasionally four journeys a day, usually well loaded on the return, and thought nothing of it. I must have grown quite tough without knowing it.

The weather cleared a bit early in October, but the rain had done much more than frighten me with mould. The summer was washed away, my extempore cardboard windowpanes were sodden and had blown in, water trickled in through the ill-fitting window frames, the roof leaked, and the discoloured patch on my new sunshine wallpaper in the bed-sitting-room had spread halfway to the floor. The writing on the wall was plain to read.

SWEET CHESTNUT

BEFORE THE LEAVES OF AUTUMN FELL I gathered sweet chestnut. The woods beckoned and I was not disobedient to their gentle summons. No more of the noisy highway and dusty lane, no more of the clink of harness or shearing of the plough, but back to the quiet glades I went, to the tall trunks and patterned aisles, to brushwood and greensward, there to work and wander, and dream of the fruitful year.

There was a quiet magic about the hush before the fall. Seed was ripened, fruit was full, new life was born. Rest and sleep were coming to the woods; and pervading the rides and brambly clearings there was a serenity and peace that beggared all telling. Work was done, nothing that was done could be undone. Life had expressed itself unstintingly, in energy and growth and sound and colour, life had made manifest in a thousand forms, and now it was all over, work was done, rest and sleep were coming.

Where white admiral and fritillary had poised and sipped so daintily now blackberries hung in dark, grape-like clusters. So black that folk often passed them by, for at a little distance there appeared to be none. When there were many reds and greens among the berries, then the trusses stood out for any child to notice, but as every fruit filled and ripened, so did the sprays droop and trail with their load, and, hanging heavy against the hedge and thicket, blended with the shadows and vanished. One particular part of the Copsford country grew blackberries extraordinary. Surely nowhere else in Sussex country did blackberries grow in such quality and quantity. It was a clearing scarcely an acre, among many young birches, in a remote spot called the Osier Beds. In the days of John Guy there had been well-tended beds of osiers, but in my day there was no trace of them except for a few old and cracked willows and two traces of swampy and impossible ground. The bramble patch was in the midst of the rather wild, unkempt young woodland that spread over the higher ground between the quagmires. It was sandy, somewhat heathy country – some eyebright grew there – and all about it bracken was on the increase. The Darn was one boundary. To most the place would have appeared a lost and wasteful wilderness, barbed with many briars, bounded by bog and brook, but to me it was a little paradise where wildlife came into its own again.

It is cause for wonder and joy the way in which wildlife floods back, like an incoming tide, to surround and submerge all men's little sand castles. In the few thousand years of his history, man has built cities and forts, ramparts and temples, roads and homes, and of many already there is no trace. Nature has crumbled them, as she is crumbling the greatest mountains. Her winds have blown over them, her seeds lodged in them, her trees and plants disrupted and covered them. Forests close their ranks. Sand drifts and buries cultivated fields and civilisations. No sooner does man take from nature one least thing to make or build some other thing than at once do forces come into play to attack, disintegrate and erase his work.

The barn and byres which had been the Copsford farm buildings had already disintegrated. In another twenty years' time there would be no recognisable trace; grass and weeds, rushes and brambles will have clothed and hidden them completely. Another fifty years, and, left alone, Copsford cottage will have disappeared likewise. As I was finding out, to my grievous discomfort, all the agents of erosion had the place on their books. Sun, wind, rain, had all been mighty busy, and I had yet to find out the activities of frost and snow. Rats had done their work, and doubtless would do much more. Walls were undermined, beams gnawed and loosened, floorboards and skirtings holed and draughty. Their filth caused rot and fungus. Plants and rubbish had blocked and choked drainpipes and airbricks, water overspilled and caused damp and mould, dry rot attacked the floorboards. Although I had driven out the devil of desertion, and swept the cottage and garnished it with many herbs, I knew only too well that the moment I should leave he would be back again, bringing with him seven others. And in this I was right, for other devils did return, and among them were hooligans, mock manoeuvres, bombs and doodlebugs.

It was the same story with the osier beds. Twenty, thirty, forty years before they had been well tended and had prospered, and a useful little local industry provided with its raw material for basketwork. Old John Guy had known all about it, and I have a fancy he had had something to do with the planting. But the tide of Victorian affairs had swept him and his craftsmen and his day off the face of the earth. How remote those times were! For it was John Guy who one day took it into his head to go and see London. He went in his smock, his brown gaiters, his tall black hat – and by the cruel thoughtfulness of one of his village cronies, with a label attached between his shoulders bearing the legend: 'This be John Guy o' Chiddinlye. Bid un welcome.' John himself told me of his visit to London of which he was very proud. 'Everybody seemed to know me,' he confided. And to the day of his death he was none the wiser. As an old gaffer told me afterwards, 'None durst tell un on it.' None indeed! John Guy was a great character, a grand character. I knew him, and, had I known of the incident at the time he was telling me about his visit – I durst not.

And since that day when the century dropped the individual I from between two quantities unknown, the osier beds were neglected. The trim-pruned pollards soon ran riot, the water ditches choked, and in a few years the beds became treacherous bogs where a false step between hummocks of razor-edged grass could plunge you thigh-deep in black mud, mantled with orange slime. The arable between the beds soon overgrew; weeds, grass, brambles and, for some unaccountable reason, birches found the light cultivated soil good, and the osier beds were only so in name. There were three clearings in my time: the first rough grass where cowslips and eyebright grew, the second a small one where the blackberries throve, the third bald and dusty where rabbits played and bracken steadily encroached.

The blackberries were magnificent, and curiously enough they were the only wild product of this land about which the farmer was especially touchy. The clearing was almost at the extreme end of his straggling territory, quite two miles from the farmhouse, and in other seasons he rarely, if ever, visited it. But when the fruit was hanging in luscious black pincushion clusters, then they were jealously guarded, and, as I soon discovered, though none too soon, a most embarrassing possession. Unfortunately, when I, quite accidentally, first stumbled across this wealth of fruit, I knew nothing whatever of the farm folks' jealous pride of ownership. I thought that I had chanced upon a place too remote for the ordinary rambler, and that that was why the fruit was in such profusion and the bushes untouched and untrampled. I gathered, without a second thought, a few pounds and found them most delicious eating. In fact they became the staple article of diet at Copsford. The berries were so fine I borrowed a basket and gathered about a dozen pounds which I proposed to offer the music mistress.

In ordinary circumstances the task of gathering a dozen pounds would have been irksome in the extreme. I hate dawdling along from hedge to hedge getting a handful here and half a dozen there, and at the end of hours of weary slogging only having to show a few miserable pounds of pippy, half-red berries. But in the osier beds things were different. This was the blackberry-pickers' dream come true. You didn't balance precariously on one foot vainly trying to reach the only respectable berry in sight, or hold the basket in one hand and stretch here and there for a couple. No, you took your stand in a little bay amongst the bushes, held the basket between your knees, and then went at the loaded bushes with both hands, just as if you were milking a cow, and picked and picked and picked. The berries were of such good quality and so full that they came off almost at a touch. One not only learnt the art of ambidextrous picking but also the art of so holding the receptacle between the knees that as the berries were picked they passed through the hands into the basket in an almost continuous stream.

It was the most satisfactory fruit-picking I have ever done in my life. There was such a show for concentrated industry, and the big basket of fine

blackberries was a goodly sight. Ten thousand pinpoints of light on purple black, multiplication and replication, every rounded fruit comprising many spheres, every sphere a spotlit pupil. They twinkle, they almost sparkle and they lie so softly compacted. Oh, how they reminded me of my grandmother's fascinating little pincushions, so closely set with glossy black-headed pins, which no doubt she – precious little lady – employed in the mysteries of fixing her lacy cap or her high black-sequin Sunday bonnet.

The music mistress was overwhelmed. By the quantity I mean; and I suppose twelve to fifteen pounds is rather a lot of blackberries to cope with, unless you are a jam- or a jelly- or a wine-maker. But she was happy to pass them on, and then I soon had requests from those who could do with them for more and more. For several days, blissfully unaware of trouble afoot, I spent busy hours in the osier beds, and must have picked some fifty pounds. Some that I picked were exposed for sale and, as luck would have it, they were seen and, without a shadow of doubt, recognised by one of the farmer's household. Then was the fat in the fire, and but for the fact that the music mistress accidentally overheard something of the shindy and passed me the tip, 'No more blackberries,' I might well have been flung ignominiously from the cottage neck and crop.

I was sorry to have caused such a storm and wanted to apologise to the farmer at once. But sometimes the furnace is too fiery even for the cold waters of regret – explosions result. It is best to wait till the fire is nearly out and then a little water may help to lay the dust.

The farmer met me as I returned to the cottage. He must have been on the lookout, for he deliberately stopped me just beyond the farmhouse. He was without the hat and looked distinctly ruffled. I felt like an erring schoolboy before his housemaster.

''Ave you seen anybody down the osier beds this day or two?' He put the question without any preamble whatever, and I wondered if I was supposed to know where the osier beds were. He had never named them to me before and I felt the question was much more dangerous than it seemed.

'The osier beds,' I murmured interrogatively. 'That's what you call that swampy bit over there, isn't it?' And I pointed vaguely in the Darn direction.

'Where them blackberries be,' eyeing me sharply.

'Blackberries,' I said, stepping warily. 'You mean up among the birches?'

'Yey! You've seed 'em I 'spect. Finest blackberries anywheres around here.'

'Yes, there are some fine ones there, ripe too. I had some for my dinner yesterday.' Like some other conspirators I felt my purple hands did reek and smoke, and should he notice them, that would be the reason.

'Yer dinner! So you 'ave been at 'em then?'

'Why, yes' – startled and apologetic – 'I-I'm sorry if I've done something wrong. I didn't know if you – that is…' Awkward pause followed.

'Finest blackberries anywheres round here,' he reiterated.

'Yes, they are indeed.' Praise seemed the only wise answer. 'And such a lot! What do you do with them?'

He scratched the back of his head at last, and I felt happier.

'There ain't no blackberries can touch 'em these parts,' he said, nodding his head emphatically.

'No,' I said, warming to the theme. 'I've never seen anything to equal them. You must be proud of them. I suppose you make them into jam or jelly or something.'

'No. We don't do nowt with 'em,' he said, somewhat puzzled, and running the fingers of his right hand through his curly grizzled hair. 'Can't abide the taste of 'em 'self.' He smiled suddenly. 'But friends we ask like 'em. Finest blackberries round here.'

'I should think so. But what's the trouble?'

'There be some — — as 'as been gettin' in there and pickin' 'em by the 'undredweight.'

'Good gracious!' I said, shocked by both language and exaggeration. 'And if ever I catches the — I'll wring 'is — neck.'

I quailed and murmured vaguely about fine blackberries.

'If you ever see anybody over them osier beds,' he continued, 'you let me know quick. I'll teach 'em.'

I said I would and he let me go. But had he guessed? Well, the time would come when no doubt we should both laugh over the incident. But the interview served its purpose. I had feigned innocence, and he had delivered the warning. Of course I left the blackberries severely alone after that, but certainly did not avoid the osier beds. And I soon noticed an extraordinary thing – great inroads *were* being made into the blackberries, both into the fruit and into the bushes. I was amazed. The farmer was right. Someone, or some persons, was stealing wholesale. I use the word stealing without blushing, for the few I gathered I took openly without any thought of hurting or robbing the farmer, whereas this thief was deliberately and secretly trespassing and taking away what must have been enormous quantities of fruit.

There followed as pretty a game of catch-as-catch-can as anyone would wish to see, and in it I joined. I did not tell the farmer that I was going to assist him keep watch for the thief. In fact my first inclinations were to keep as far from the osier beds as possible, for I felt as guilty as a runaway ring whenever I went near the place. But my discovery that there was a real pilferer made me determined to find out who it was. So at considerable risk I would creep by devious ways into the osier beds to watch what happened. It was thrilling work, worming one's way through the bracken, creeping on hands and knees through the bushes, wading the brook, slipping dangerously across the swamp, once to slide into the ooze till the black mud squelched about my waist. Hunters, unbeknownst to one another, hunted, and the hunted hunted the hunters.

My five months' intensive training in quiet woodcraft stood me in good stead, and I had learnt to be still, as quiet and inconspicuous as a woodcock in the tangle. I had learnt just a little of that amazing world, that body, that complexity of wildlife which, with all its delicate actions, interactions and reactions, is more sensitive to behaviour, foreign to its nature, than the most exact, intricate or elaborate instrument that we could ever dream of. As I gradually became aware of it I was reminded of that imponderable, all-pervading ether about which we were taught at school and which, although altogether intangible, is nevertheless capable of taking stresses and strains and transmitting them through its medium with the velocity of light to the uttermost ends of creation.

In the world of wildlife the stresses and strains which the whims and works of men imposed did not travel with the speed of light, but travel they certainly did, and one did not have to journey to the last island universe to see their effects, for everywhere about there were sensitive detectors which received and instantaneously retransmitted information received. But besides transmission there was also transformation into new sound or new language or new movement. The original impact might have been no more than the sight of a man slipping stealthily across an open glade, but instantly some part of the life complex is aware of it, perhaps a wood pigeon, which leaves the edge of the clearing with a clap of wings. Two or three others immediately follow and they speed away from the point of disturbance and make for the marsh. A carrion crow spies their movement and, at once suspicious, cries harshly from his lookout on the tip-top of a tall alder. A mate of his immediately responds from his vantage a hundred yards downstream, and his sudden rough bark startles a blackbird which speeds noisily through the birches and makes a wren somewhere in the blackberry thicket beside me scold angrily.

It reads crudely on paper, but when one lies in the bosom of the wild and feels the tender rise and fall of her breathing, the magic of life's response defies description. One feels as well as sees and hears. Suddenly one becomes aware that something has happened, something is occurring which is different from rabbits gambolling in the clearing, or jays squabbling in the copse, or bank voles playing submarines in the brook. One is not conscious of having noticed any one thing in particular, yet the alert has sounded. There is an indefinable tension, reaction to a distant stress, and one's ears prick and one's breathing checks and one listens and observes with acute attention.

I lay like a log in the yellowing bracken, and wondered if some slight chance movement of mine had caught the inquisitive eye of the little wren, all was so still. But through the screen of grasses and tall stems I could see two rabbits had ceased their play and one was sitting erect, kangaroo-like, alert with ears, eyes and nose. I could see the twitching of its sensitive nostrils, and I wished that I had the power to read the information in the breeze as it did. I could smell the warm pungent odour of the bracken and the sweet purple scent of blackberries, and, hanging in the air, was the first fragrance of autumn, but of what came on the wind from a distance I knew nothing. I watched the rabbits. One still sat alert, frozen, like a little garden image of stone. Suddenly eyes, ears and nose all seemed to look in one direction. I too tried to peer, but the fern was too close about me to see anything, if there was anything to see. Yet when I glanced back at the rabbits to glean further information from them they had vanished.

The tension increased. I heard the frit of a dragonfly's wings as it darted overhead. Normally I should have let its movement pass unnoticed, but now I was convinced it had been disturbed from its usual beat along the bushes near the swamp. There had been a party of tits high overhead foraging in the tops of the birches; I could not see them, but I had heard their little social notes. I could distinguish a change in their cries. They were sharper and there were scolds, then they drifted away. Some magpies set up a chattering down by the brook, and I heard the shrill 'kraah' of a moorhen. Then without the least warning, like someone tearing a piece of tough fabric in a silent room, a jay rent the quiet of the clearing with his sharp scream – I heard the stiff whistle of his wings as he swept low overhead, and I knew, and all the clearing knew, that danger was at hand.

Whoever was coming was approaching very stealthily, and though I longed to stand up and catch the first glimpse of the trespasser, I dared not, for fear he was well hid and should see me first. Like Brer Fox, I lay low. I felt uncomfortably alone. The little wren had fled, other birds had followed the jay, the tits had gone, and the rabbits, after stamping their warning, had disappeared underground. It was very still. I was evidently in the midst of the disturbance, in the centre of the cyclone. There was a slight rustle, and scarce daring to turn my head, I saw a mouse, a field vole, dodging through the tangle of grasses and towering stems of the bracken as an orchid hunter might force his way through the forests of the Amazon. It lightly crossed my legs and hurried away. If the mouse had been disturbed by the intruder, he must be very near, I thought, and almost at the same moment I heard a brushing in the fern. The thief was crawling through within a few yards of me.

My heart leapt, and then beat almost to suffocation. I lay pressed to earth like a partridge, expecting every second that he would stumble across me. But no, the rustle of his passage was a little to my left, and then, just as I thought he would break cover, the noise ceased. He too lay close in the bracken and waited. It was as good as a detective story, and I lost all count of time in the excitement. We might have lain there for minutes or tens of minutes, when fortunately for me the tension was eased by the noisy approach of the farmer himself. He was no woodsman, or if he was he certainly did not show it, for he came noisily through the birches, snapping twigs and startling all and sundry around him.

I could not help smiling as I lay with my face pressed to the earth; it would have read such an excellent chapter in the thriller. And I could have sprung out from the bracken as the farmer passed within a few yards and exposed the real thief there and then before his startled eyes. It would have been a first-rate climax. But finesse appeals to me more than grand slams. I lay low and said nothing, and his boots dragged roughly through the brambles just ahead of me. He passed, muttering, occasionally striking the bushes with a stick as if he were drawing the coverts, but he got no view. He circled the clearing and gradually the noise of his passage died away in the direction it had come. Quiet returned, and wildlife, deceived by the audible and visible departure of a man, returned also. As we lay in the bracken it flowed back over us. Birds, rabbits, insects, voles, streamed back into the natural channels of their lives. We created no stress as we crouched motionless among the fern, but instead resembled high potential charges ready to leap the spark-gap and set the ether violently vibrating to a new disturbance.

How I wondered what was passing in the mind of that other lying there so near me. Would he ever budge? Had he been shaken by the arrival of the farmer? It had, I suppose, been a close shave for him. If he had gone straight to his picking, he might well have been spotted, if not caught, though I fancied he was too quick-witted and too sharp-eared to be seen, let alone caught. Whenever would he move? A mosquito sang menacingly near my ear. I hated the sound of its pinging whine and feared it would settle on my face, for I dared not move, so silent was the brake. But it winged mournfully away and I lost sight of it, till suddenly I was conscious of a sharp tiny twinge in my finger, and there was the little brute with its vicious proboscis buried deep in my flesh and its hind legs waving in drunken delight. It is not much good knocking off or crushing a mosquito once it has pierced you. Some folks say it will draw much of its irritating poison out again if allowed to drink your blood to the full. I watched it, and it was a queer and unpleasantly exciting sensation to feel it extracting one's blood. And not only to feel but to see! Slowly its body – its abdomen, began to swell. It swelled and swelled till it became tight and transparent, its little yellow-striped, stick-like belly became a swollen, pear-shaped drop of blood. My

blood! Much incensed, I was about to squash it with my thumb when my
attention was distracted by the cry of a green woodpecker. It came from
somewhere on the other side of the blackberry clearing. There was nothing
very unusual in this, even though it was autumn. Yet was there something
about that laughing whistle, something just a little unusual that jarred my
attention? I had scarcely pondered a couple of seconds when to my intense
astonishment the same shrill cry came from the bracken beside me!

So that was it, there were two of them. And that set me thinking
furiously. Had that other been there even before I arrived? Did he know
that I was there? Had I, in my long arduous crawl, been incautious, and
shown myself, I wondered? I hoped not, and I racked my brains in an effort
to remember any stress or strain that might have been caused by another. I
could think of nothing. There was a second call from the other side which
was followed at once by a rustling in the bracken near me. They were on
the move. With infinite caution I raised my head, not above he bracken, but
just above the jungle of grasses so that I might peer among those pillared
stems that supported the ferny roof. But the sound of movement was not
towards the clearing – they were on the retreat. Exasperated at the thought
that, after all my exertions and patience, a sight of the thief should escape
me, I took the risk of half sitting up in a last effort to catch a glimpse of him.
But the bracken was very thick; I despaired, when suddenly, down a long
avenue such as sometimes unexpectedly occurs, owing perhaps to an old
track or rabbit run, I caught one fleeting glimpse of an incautiously raised
head – the back of a head, uncovered, long-haired. It was a young woman.

Had I seen that hair before?

It had been such a shock of surprise to me that the thief, or the accomplice,
was a woman, that, in the brief two seconds that the head was in my view, I
scarcely seemed to take in more than that it was female. But afterwards, in
those minutes, hours, days, that followed, I was tantalised almost beyond
bearing by trying to recall in precise detail exactly what I had seen.

It is always so easy to superimpose afterthoughts. At first I was certain that
I had recognised the hair, that I had actually seen it among the household
at the farm. Afterwards I began to doubt. It was altogether too much like

sensational detective fiction, and, after all, one woman's uncovered head is very much like another. I reached that stage when I doubted whether I had ever seen anything at all. Had I dozed in the sun? Had a woodpecker awakened me and this was my waking dream?

When doing a jigsaw puzzle one often confidently picks up a piece which both in shape and colour seems exactly the bit for which one has been looking, only to find, on applying it to the cavity, that it is a misfit. Experts, on the other hand, often fit a piece into the puzzle, having recognised the right shape even though the piece was upside down. I was no expert. To me it had suddenly seemed that I had a piece to fit in the blackberry mystery. Colour, pattern, shape, all appeared to match. It explained so much that was curious about the affair that for long periods I accepted it as a certain fit. Then doubt and reaction followed and I was equally certain that such an improbable solution could never be. My investigations into the great blackberry mystery ended there. I never expected to spy on a woman, and because I was under the shadow of suspicion, from which I could not escape unless I exploded a depth charge under someone else, it left an unpleasant taste in my mouth. I was glad when the finches had finished off the last of the withered, seedy fruits.

Blue-bloomed sloes tasted less bitter than the blackberries. How lovely they looked – strings and clusters of little grapes among the thorns, and how they shrivelled my tongue whenever I ventured to taste them! And there were those fantastic girdles and necklaces of the green, orange and scarlet berries of black bryony, so alluring to the eyes and so repulsive to the palate. Everywhere the hedges were decked with their white, withering strands, on which, like polished beads, were strung the glossy fruits. There they hung, untouched, till frost and rain destroyed them. It was not so with the haws. Birds greedily devoured them long before the stern days of winter famine arrived. I was astonished to see the way in which blackbirds, thrushes and missel thrushes stripped the hawthorns, that is, certain hawthorns, perhaps those with a particularly favoured flavour, or maybe those that ripened early, while other loaded bushes were left severely alone for a time. Then came the great influx of fieldfares and redwings, and travelling parties of hawfinches, and soon all my glowing thorns had lost their fire.

I dawdled over the gathering of sweet-chestnut leaves. Not only was it my last harvest but the woods were so exquisitely lovely and the autumnal atmosphere so golden and yellow that linger I must. I would pick a bagful almost as light as a feather-filled pillow, and on some sun-dappled knoll recline with my back against it and fall into timeless contemplation. I saw without looking. I heard without listening. I perceived without reasoning. I became a part of the woods. The long hush of the midday breeze whispered about me and in it I heard the response of ten thousand choirs of tiny voices. It was the slow movement, the andante, of a great choral symphony in which all the muted strings quivered in tremulous spiccato, and the voices came sigh upon sigh, soft, pianissimo, loud, appassionato, wave on wave, advancing, receding, flooding in, and then rippling and all a-shimmer, like the trembling surface of a lake alive with evening light.

With the first sharp November frosts the leaves fell.

They showered down in inconceivable multitudes. The slightest breath of air seemed as though it must denude the trees to the very last twig. But there were always more, and the next chilly draw of frosty air brought another twinkling shower of greens and yellows, gold and bronze, brown and crimson. I could never restrain the impulse to dart among the shower and catch a falling leaf. As a small boy I had whimsically been taught that there was magic in a falling leaf, if you caught it before it touched the ground. Many an autumn morning a little fellow darted hither and thither beneath some rugged elm, and in exciting chase danced and sprang after those fantastic, elusive, aerial acrobats, those golden leaves chat turned and twisted, glanced and glided, swerved and somersaulted just out of reach. Oh, but the exultation of a capture! That was a rich prize indeed, to be held tight in a tiny fist, to be taken indoors and exhibited with pride, its potent magic to be reassessed. Perfect mothers understand. Forty years on and I still cannot resist a capture; and is there not, in fact, magic enough in a single leaf for our minds to conjure with? Did not a child learn from them something of the soul of a tree, of its sturdy strength, its steadfastness and courage, its open arms and friendly welcome, its voice awakened with every wind? A tree is an individual life, and wherever there is life we may apprehend ideas, the ideas of the Creator.

November also brought the farmer's cart to Copsford. The portcullis was raised, the bridge cleared, and with some noise of shouting, my precious sacks, bulging, sewn and labelled, made the hazardous journey from the drying room of the cottage to guard's van in the station. No one could have watched over their merchandise with a more motherly eye than I my fragrant bags. That it might rain or the day be dirty was my constant anxiety. That the bags might burst, under the rough and oh-so-callous handling of the porters and farmer, almost drove me frantic. It was like watching one's children manhandled by strangers. It jarred me to see my hard-won treasure flung from cart to road, sweet agrimony, crisp meadowsweet, fragrant centaury, lumped, jolted, bundled with less ceremony than sacks of potatoes. I wished with distracted heart that I had never had to part with them. All my patient work, all my joyous experience, all my golden hours in the sunshine, my baptism in the waters of freedom, my happy memories of beloved birds and insects, trees and flowers, seemed to be stored in that medley of sacks.

They were flung on the weighing machine, and with a seemingly careless flick of a ridiculously small slider, the precious pounds were casually announced and jotted down on the back of a dirty envelope: 60 lb, 48 lb, 73 lb, 29 lb... many weights and many sizes. Then the total, that took some reckoning, but after several efforts the sum was agreed to within a few pounds. And was it farm produce? Well, was it? I said it was herbs, and was regarded somewhat suspiciously. But it was, and at last 'farm produce' it was decided to be. It made a considerable difference to my slender pocket, and allowed for a substantial tip to the guard, with whom I pleaded that my children should not be left anywhere exposed to the weather. He was a good fellow and my trust in him was not betrayed.

Then slowly back to the cottage. My footsteps sounded hollow and echoing as I entered. Copsford was empty.

A Jay in the clearing

ACCOUNTS

THE HERB HARVEST WAS OVER. There was no work for me to do in the woods and fields. There would be no more gathering until next April or May. Long empty months stretched before me, and I began to wonder not only if I could endure them lonely and inactive, but if my means would bridge them. The time had indeed come when I should have to render an account to the gentleman in the room upstairs; and I dreaded doing it.

For nearly eight months I had lived a carefree gypsy life, spending nothing except on the barest necessities. Small sums of money had trickled in during that time, partly from freelance journalism, partly from small quantities of fresh herbs which I was fortunate enough to have been requested to supply. But they were very mall, and any extra expense such as the perpetual stove in the drying room and its paraffin, or the cost of putting the herbs on rail and tipping the guard was a serious matter, and made the week's account borrow from the past or the future.

Living in the country was much cheaper than living in the town. For the third-floor-back I had to pay 14s. 6d. a week, plus gas. For Copsford I had to pay 3s. a week and find methylated and oil for the primus. In London I had usually to buy a lunch out, while in the country I prepared all my own meals how and when I liked. In town, milk and butter were expensive, but from the farm I had all the milk I needed for a penny a day, farm butter sixpence a week, and eggs a penny each. The minimum cost of living off King's Street,

Chelsea, was 28s. a week; the minimum in the country, 10s.

But in London I had spent my whole time writing and I had been able to meet the bill. At Copsford I had spent my whole time harvesting and had hardy been able to meet the bill. However, the return for my herbs had not yet come in, and it was for that cheque that I was waiting before I presented my balance sheet. But though I needed it sorely I dreaded its coming. So much depended upon it.

The prices of herbs fluctuate even more than they do for most farm produce. Imports from the Continent vary enormously in quantity, with the result that home-grown herbs may one season be 6d. or 8d. per lb, and the next be 1s. or 1s. 6d. There is also a very variable demand, and, what may have been popular for a few years, slumps quite suddenly and there may be no sale for it for a longer time than it would be worth keeping. Furthermore there is the quality of the harvested herb itself. Really good stuff, gathered at the right time and in the right conditions, dried and stored in the proper manner, entirely free from adulteration, can command a very much better price than poor and discoloured and weedy stuff. In fact it may be the only herb that will sell in an overloaded year.

While waiting for the prices, I began to jot down what it had cost me to live in Copsford for eight months. The account was as follows:

	£	s.	d.
Rent @ 3/– per week	5	0	0
Butter, milk, eggs @ 1/3	2	2	0
Bread @ 1/6	2	10	0
Groceries @ 3/–	5	0	0
Paraffin and meth. @ 1/6	2	10	0
Sundries, dog biscuits, etc @ 6d.	1	16	0
Total	£18	18	0

These figures appear quite ridiculous by modern, postwar standards. Friends have declared that it would be impossible to live on six or seven shillings a week. Yet it was possible because I did it, and not for two or three

weeks, but for ten months. Provided one has plenty of bread, butter, milk
and eggs, there is no need for much else except for variety. I never bought
a piece of meat the whole time I lived in the cottage, because, of course, I
had no means of roasting it. All my cooking was done on the primus. Frying
was my high-water mark, bacon, eggs, mushrooms, with potatoes or bread,
being the dish *par excellence*, eaten piping hot, straight from the pan. I never
dabbled with pudding-making or suchlike cooking. I really had not the time
and inclination, let alone the ingredients and utensils. Popular breakfast
cereals, tinned goods, sugar, tea and dog biscuits were the groceries I bought.

The music mistress must have perceived the skimpiness of my larder when
she paid her visit to the cottage, for after that she frequently made for me a
large flat cake, meat-dish size, which lasted me many days, and was a most
welcome addition to all meals. She did, too, in her thoughtful and practical
way, put aside special bones for Floss, who was just as grateful as I was. I'm
afraid my fare did not leave much for a dog, and Floss had to subsist very
largely on dog biscuits.

At last the cheque arrived. I picked it up with my other mail at the post
office, but I did not open it. Not till I was back in Copsford and seated in the
only chair in the upper room did I slowly slit the envelope. The cheque was
drawn for £34: 4: 2. The price list was as follows:

	£	s.	d.
Clivers, 120 lb @ 6d.	3	0	0
Foxglove, 48 lb @ 1/3	3	2	0
Centaury, 29 lb @ 1/–	1	9	0
Agrimony, 206 lb @ 1/	11	2	3
Meadowsweet, 153 lb @ 8d.	5	2	0
Tansy, 42 lb @ 9d.	1	11	6
Eyebright, 23 lb @ 1/6	1	14	6
Yarrow, 148 lb @ 9d.	5	11	0
Chestnut, 36 lb @ 11d.	1	13	0
Total	£34	4	2

I sat staring out of the uncurtained window for a long time. The countryside
was empty and bare. The hedges were leafless, the woods toneless and stark,
the rough meadows flowerless and dull with withering grasses. All the
abundant life and luxuriant foliage of the spring and summer seemed to
have come to naught. All my work, my care, my gathering, my journeying,
one year of my life, seemed to have shrunk to no more than this little slip
of coloured paper folded between my fingers. Not that I was disappointed

with the value of the cheque – far from it. After the slender income of the past months it was affluence. But it was the fact that all my experiences, all my struggles, all my triumphs, should be summed up as so much cash, that discomforted me. To receive money for all those labours somehow seemed hopelessly inadequate, a pathetic anticlimax. The labour had been so worthwhile. I had worked, how I had worked, often sixteen hours a day. But I had enjoyed it. I had found immense pleasure in toiling among the wild things of the countryside, in brushing through the dense herbage of the marsh, stooping in the blazing sun among the agrimony, stealing through the shadowy woodland, returning loaded with great bales to the aromatic cottage. I had been heart and soul in my task and what one gives one's life to can only be rewarded by fabulous sums or nothing. My work was ended, and it was valued at £34: 4: 2.

What wonder I sat staring out of the window! Copsford was a suitable place to muse on the intrinsic value of things. Those herbs, whether they were to be used for medicinal or culinary purposes, whether they were to be tonic or tobacco, seemed to me beyond price. They were the sweet plants of our English countryside. They had grown there, each in its own peculiar habitat, rich in sunshine and shadow, rain and the good earth. They had been gathered with toil, harvested with patience, stored and dispatched with care. Yet their market value was only a few pence a pound. Did those who ultimately bought them, I wondered, benefit to the extent of a handful of copper, or did they receive the riches which I fancied in them were stored?

Floss whimpered and poked her wet nose into my palm. Poor dog. Good dog. This was not like the days with which she had grown familiar. As I patted her she put her head on my knee and oogled at me in the way dogs do when they sense a change of mood. Or did she in that mood perceive forebodings? Did she see the shadow of things to come fall across that slip of paper which she nudged from my fingers so that it fell on the floor? She pushed in closer after its departure, and the tassel of her tail flickered with pleasure as she felt she now had my whole attention. Good dog, good dog! How simple are your solutions! Why should not I ignore it altogether, let it lie there, let it slip through the floorboards?

But I picked it up, I could not afford heroics. I went back to the account. The prices of the herbs were on the whole satisfactory. While clivers at 6*d.* per lb and centaury at only 1*s.* were very poor, agrimony on the other hand at 1*s.* 1*d.* was good, and fortunately coincided with my largest harvest. Yarrow at 9*d.* and meadowsweet at 8*d.* were both good, so that I considered on the average my prices were higher than I had expected.

There was another account to render. It ran as follows:

	£	s.	d.
Literary work:			
Regular monthly feature	1	8	0
Sundry contributions	16	9	6
	£24	9	6
Added to this the herbs I sold fresh	3	15	0
	£28	4	6
Added to this, cheque as above	34	4	2
Making a grand total gross income of	£62	8	8
From this I had to deduct what it had cost me to live for 8 months	£18	18	0
And sundry emergency expenses such as the store house, stove, etc	1	15	6
Total	£20	13	6

This by simple subtraction showed me to be worth £41 : 15 : 2.

It was immensely satisfactory on paper. Floss audited it with a muddy paw mark, and applauded with much yapping as the senior director, chairman, manager, & Co. got stiffly out of his chair. Yes, I should be able to bridge the gap, even though cost of living in the winter should be double that in the summer.

But oh, how pitifully small the return really was!

And was I getting anywhere?

Thus by slow degrees I came to the balance sheet. But both assets and liabilities were weighted with unknown and imponderable quantities, and it was beyond my skill to strike it. At school I never had been any good at book-keeping. Many painful interviews had only succeeded in teaching me Trade Account and Profit and Loss. I am ashamed to say that the balance sheet was completely beyond me. Wholesale cribbing and the headmaster's fury were not enlightening, and to this day its jargon and jugglery confound me. Small wonder the Copsford account was distracting. I attempted to weigh the imponderable.

I contemplated another year at the cottage. No doubt I would do much better next year. I knew where herbs grew. I would not have to waste time searching. I could go further afield. I could dry artificially in damp weather, and thus clear my drying rooms quicker. I could sell some of the first harvests earlier, probably at a better price, and have more space in my storerooms beside reducing the risks of loss owing to mould or deterioration. I knew the business better in every way, and I had already a small connection. But suppose I doubled my return, suppose I trebled it – which considering the immense amount of gathering it would entail was extremely doubtful – was I really getting anywhere? I had to consider also the possibility of a poor summer, or low prices, or disability to gather, or – a new cloud on the horizon – the farmer wanting the cottage, for my tenancy had gradually altered his attitude towards Copsford. It had begun to appear to him as a place more useful than he had imagined. He might, very cheaply, put a labourer in to help him. Coupled to this there was within me an ever-increasing tension which, as I said at first, exists in every human being, the tension between the gregarious instinct and the solitary. After nearly a year alone I needed company. I loved the wild countryside, and as long as I was about and busy in it, all was well. But as soon as I was cooped up and idle, but for my pen, I was miserable, and craved to be out and doing, or else to be among my own kind.

But a decision had to be made, and while Floss and I went for the milk from the farm, I determined to remain at Copsford, at any rate to complete the year and see the winter through.

Copsford gave me its last
rich gift—Winter Glory

WINTER

It rained with fury and persistence. The Darn filled up and frothed along, muddy and turbulent.

The sodden fields squelched and spurted water at every step, the barways became mud bogs where, in wellingtons, one dare not cross for fear of losing a boot sucked off in the mire. Copsford, exposed to the full force of the wind, streamed water within and without. It was in a sorry plight. The roof drains, blocked with the rubbish of years, literally foamed at the mouth. The wind seemed to drive the water clean through the walls which glistened and streamed with moisture. Pools gathered on the floors of the upper rooms, and trickled through the cracks in the boards and caused great discoloured patches on the grey ceilings below, which themselves began to drip. My improvised cardboard windows were quickly sodden and blown to pieces. I had to fix boards to restrain the violence of the wind, which was hurling gouts of water clean across the room. Downstairs I attempted to secure an old sheet of corrugated iron outside the small window which faced south. Few tasks could be more maddening.

It is strange how quickly and how completely bemused one becomes when battling with the elements. When you struggle against a violent gale, or wrestle with mountainous seas, or beat through torrential rain, or are overtaken by a wild blizzard, or attempt a stern climb in rough and dangerous weather, you begin to lose all sense of proportion. The task in hand becomes tremendous, little else seems to matter, conditions are distorted, expectations violently exaggerated; you seem to be at the centre of a world going mad. Perhaps there is going to be another flood; perhaps the snow will last for weeks and the countryside be blotted out and a new ice age be ushered in; perhaps – but there is no end to the fantastic ideas which seem to spring up in the mind. Not only does one imagine oneself to be in the throes of a superhuman struggle, but one is conscious of a sense of exaltation, of joy in the midst of distress, of pride at the thought of fame.

But the rain ceases, the wind drops, the snow thins, and the world is as it was before, and nothing stupendous whatever has happened. Yet somehow we do not fall so very flat, we only wonder at people's lack of imagination in failing to perceive the greatness of our struggle.

It is absurd, often quite amusing, for we ourselves are just as unimaginative and completely fail to appreciate the tremendous adventure of those who for the first time were caught for half an hour in a smother of cloud on the mountainside. To them, when they lost the way and found themselves on the verge of a seething cloud-filled abyss, it was as though they faced eternity; to us below in the sunlit valley it was no more than the very common sight of cloud down on the crags. If anyone from a detached, dry, sheltered position had been able to watch me fight with that sheet of corrugated iron, they would, I am sure, have laughed till their sides ached. But to me it was a most savage encounter. For an old piece of corrugated iron in a high wind is a most unmanageable and horrible thing. Its edges are rusty, broken and sharp. It catches the wind like the sail of a yacht. It is unbalanced whichever way you pick it up, and if you carry it in front of you, you cannot see where you are going. I had attempted to carry the piece from the ruins of the barn, but the wind immediately whipped it round, tore it from my hands and flung it on to the ground so that I stumbled against it and cut a gash in trousers, socks and calf. With the rain lashing me and running down inside my collar, and my old coat – the last button having burst away under the strain – flapping and thrashing around me, I became, as described above, completely bemused. I fought a Quixotic battle with a giant in corrugated mail. I grappled, I wrestled. It sprang from my grasp and then leapt at me with all the fury of the gale behind it. I dodged just in time as it angled past me like an enormous knife. It slapped to the ground with a dash like concert thunder, and lay shamming dead; and the rain spattered noisily upon it, like a vigorous second refreshing its champion.

No sooner was it up than it poured muddy rivers down its beastly corrugations and filled my boots with mud and bloody water. I was mad and could see nothing but life or death in the fixing of the thing outside that window. We strove amain. I got it up on end and was just heaving it into position when a side gust took it and jabbed it viciously into the top left-hand pane of the window. Glass flew in all directions, and I'm afraid I swore both loud and deep. At it again, and we had a spell of vicious in-fighting, until it slipped under my guard and a little rosette of jagged points, surrounding a nail-hole, sliced a rent in my coat ten inches long. It was a mean trick and only served to infuriate me further. Awaiting a brief lull in the gale, I suddenly pounced upon it when it was not looking and forced it violently into position. Triumph! I bent down to seize a heavy batten which I was to use as a prop to hold the iron in place when a furious gust of wind wrenched it from the wall and hurled it down upon me. Off my balance and overweighted with the timber, I just crumpled up under the blow and took the count on the sodden ground. Certainly everything went dark, but no doubt that was because I was underneath the iron. I do not remember much more except that at length I crawled, weak and wet, into the cottage, and as for that damned corrugated, it may be lying there yet for all I care.

That night the wind veered and by morning the rain had changed to sleet, and the sleet changed to snow, and before the next nightfall Copsford stood grim and chill in a pallid loneliness. Nothing isolates one more than snow and Arctic cold, and as I left the farmhouse and trudged wearily across the mantled fields I felt like a polar explorer who has turned his back on the last food depot and set out alone on his fantastic quest.

I had left the village late, and by the time I had picked up my milk and water it was pitch dark. Normally snow on the ground reflects sufficient light to see by under the cloudiest skies, but that night I could scarce see the snow at my feet. It was still snowing furiously and the moonless heavens must have been choked with snow clouds. I was compelled to borrow a storm lantern. The way to Copsford was as familiar to my feet as the way up the stairs, but on that amazing night I could not find it. I blundered along in more than six inches of snow and got completely lost. I held the lantern aloft, but its feeble glow could not pierce the swirling, flying frenzy of snowflakes. All it did was to illuminate what seemed a sphere of confusion, a globe of ten thousand darting, dancing, streaking lines of light.

On my grandmother's what-not in the best drawing room there had stood a wonderful globe of glass containing a liquid which made it appear as a crystal ball. Magically imprisoned within it was a little scene: a house, a garden, a tree and a tiny figure. On rare red-letter days I used to be allowed to approach this miracle, and then to my astonished and delighted childish eyes the ball was inverted and replaced and instantly within it raged a tremendous and tempestuous snowstorm. As for most English children, who only get their winter in small doses, snow had an irresistible fascination for me. I longed for it almost as madly as I longed for the coming of Christmas Day itself. The sight of a few stray flakes drifting across the garden would cause me to spring to my feet and shout exultingly, 'It's snowing!' And although those sailing feathers vanished no sooner than they touched the ground, nevertheless my child's mind leapt into a transformed world, and all that I had seen on Christmas cards, in Christmas annuals, and in particular in my favourite book, *The Arctic Regions*, which contained many absorbing pictures of icebergs and igloos, walrus and eskimo, blue night resplendent with the aurora borealis, became vivid possibilities. 'It's snowing!' The cry had an electric effect. My young brother and I would rush out into the garden and pray to and plead with Mother Goose to hasten with her plucking and send more and yet more of the downy breast our way.

It is still the same, and always will be: children love a snowfall. They nudge one another in school, they see the fascinating white lines streaking past the classroom window, their eyes shine, they jump up and down in their desks, the tense whisper circulates, 'It's snowing!' And as the ground whitens and the ceiling takes on a strange unearthly glare, the excitement rises, till on the bell they burst from the door and partake of all the joy and woe of a snowball battle.

The globe on the what-not epitomised all that and much more, and, as I struggled through the blizzard towards the Darn, vainly holding aloft the hurricane lantern in an endeavour to discover one recognisable landmark, I suddenly realised that one of my childish dreams had there and then come true. I was that little figure inside the globe. As I floundered, so the lantern cast a grotesque and gigantic shadow of myself upon the outside of the sphere of flying flakes with which I was by light imprisoned; and by a strange inversion, I, the puny figure within, thus saw projected an enormous phantom of myself without, whereas in those far-off childhood days I, without, had imagined myself the Lilliputian figure within.

At length I found the Darn and worked my way along it till I found the barricaded bridge. Thence up the hill I could not go far wrong, and within a few moments of my shrill whistle Floss found me, and like a good team from the St Bernard we came safely to our cell. But Copsford was no place for a lodging on a night like that. There was indeed shelter from biting wind and stinging snow but the place was as cold as the grave. On an eddy of wind, snow had piled in the open front door and curved like a frozen wave across the threshold. Through a hole in the scullery window, fine flakes had come drifting and lay in broad unmelted sweep right across the cold brick floor. Floss's paw marks were imprinted freshly in it. She had evidently been trying to keep warm upon the bed, where she had heard my whistle and had come careering down the stairs and leapt the drift at the front door to come and find me. No room was without snow somewhere within it. Yet I would not and could not retrace my steps to the farm or village; something must be done, and quickly before Floss and I were frozen chill or driven silly by the shrill and moan of the icy wind.

I had never yet burnt a fire in the great tumbledown fireplace, but now I was determined to do so whatever happened, and with wrapping paper and odd lengths of board began a blaze which startled Copsford from foundations to chimney. My word, how it crackled and sparked! A good deal of smoke and flame billowed out into the room, and more blackening and blisters were added to the ancient mantelshelf; but it did our eyes good to see the blaze, and the light of the storm lantern paled and yellowed before it. But board wood did not last long in a furnace like that, and very soon my stock of fuel was consumed. I toured the cottage with the storm lantern for more, but beyond a little blockade material there was nothing. It meant that to keep ourselves alive we should have to brave the blast again and search amid the snow-buried ruins of the barn for more fuel.

I struggled into my snow-caked coat, now frozen like a coat of mail, and with Floss immensely excited, went forth into the wild night to gather winter fuel. No King Wenceslas brought me pine logs, but in nearly a foot of snow and by the light of a flickering lantern the dog and I rummaged in search of old timber. Fortunately I knew the wreckage pretty well and was able to lay my hands on, or rather kick my feet into, some sizeable pieces which in earlier days I had heaped together for possible constructional purposes. My hands were so numb I could scarcely close my fingers and I cannot altogether recollect how we managed to drag the wood to the cottage. In the nightmare of whirling snow and stumbling drifts I simply remember the amazing sight of a ruddy glow in the window and across the snow from the open door, as each time I found the cottage; and I recalled too with a warm heart, and that indeed was all that was warm within me, the bounding, shadowy form of Floss as she leapt in and out of the lantern light, and her fiery guiding eyes as she beckoned to me from the confines of that circle of confusion.

With a considerable pile of sodden, snow-covered wood flung across the floor, I was at length satisfied, and kicking out the drifted snow, propped the door shut. Then I built up such a fire as would have satisfied the bonfire-makers of Lewes. I had nothing with which to cut up the longer pieces, so the ends of these were thrust in the blaze and the fire shortened them. Other pieces I pushed up the chimney and these too automatically dwindled. As it was, the great cavity, which had once contained a kitchen range, would take pieces four or five feet long, so that between my improvised firedogs I was able to support some goodly chunks, worm-pocked rafters, tarry boards, rotted posts and broken beams. I suffered exquisite agony as my extremities thawed, and so, I think, did Floss, for she whimpered a little and licked and bit her paws, and shook her ears, and made sudden convulsive movements as though her joints hurt her. But the fire was good. There is nothing like fire to revive the drooping spirit. There must be something in fire akin to the human mind. Who is not attracted to a great consuming blaze? Do not beacons on the hills rouse the spirit of a nation with their roaring fiery tongues?

Fire! That should have been the proper end of Copsford. So I imagined as I huddled in my chair, draped in blankets and with Floss upon my knees. Now and again as I stared dreamily into the furnace a log end would fall with a crash and a great shower of sparks go hurtling up the cavernous chimney. What, I wondered, did that stark stack look like spouting fire? But who was there to see? Copsford was as isolated as a whaler caught in the Antarctic ice. If Copsford blazed like a beacon with gouts of flame belching from every shattered window, who on that tempestuous night would see or know or care? Who sees the fires of Erebus? Only Floss and I would see that volcanic end when the roof fell in and the last dramatic shower of sparks burst upwards and mingled with the fire-flushed snow.

Drowsing thus at length I woke, and there was my great fire no more than a heap of snowy ash about my feet. The lantern had gone out, but there was a cold light about the room, and, though I was so stiff from my cramped position in the chair that I could scarcely turn my head, I could see that the big window was slubbered up with ice. The cottage was deadly quiet, the wind had died away. I tried slowly to move and had a moment's horror that something had happened to me because I could not free my arms. It was, however, only one of the blankets which had become tight swathed around me, and I was thankful to be loosed from it. The other, with Floss, had slipped to the floor and she was tight curled up in it. One edge of the blanket was badly charred by a log fallen from the fire. That was as near as we had come to Erebus.

Floss woke the moment I moved my feet, and gradually we stirred ourselves to life and movement, Floss with a shrill yawn and a long stretching of forepaws, I with stamping feet and massaging neck. The first thing was to light the fire up again and get the primus going, then we dared to unprop the front door and inspect.

A curl of drifted snow fell in upon our feet. But we cared not about it for the scene before our eyes was magical. A fragment of the old moon still glittered in the east. It glittered from the violet-and-purple band that zoned the wintry sky. Above this band to the zenith was a bowl of deepest blue, pinpointed with fading stars. Beneath it to the white horizon another belt of brighter blue, frosty and clear, and just crimsoning below the moon. And on every hand the superb mantle of driven snow, pure and sparkling.

We stared. Neither drift nor cold, nor fire nor smoke, could drag our eyes away. Of course I speak for myself; but Floss stared too, with nose lifted and alive, and ears just folded back, and I wonder what she saw? Did she see the sheer beauty of that wintry morning? Dogs have a way of standing on high places and staring away to far horizons as if they contemplated something that satisfied them. I often thought Floss gazed at things as if perceiving beauty. Perhaps dogs do, feeling it rather than comprehending it. She broke the spell at length, bounding over the drift and then jumping and floundering about in the powdery pile in the greatest of high spirits. I returned and made thick smoky toast before the re-kindled fire, and after making tea, sat warm and comforted, contemplating that most satisfying and cheering sight – a kettle boiling for dear life, pouring clouds of coiling steam from its jolly mouth and chuckling beneath its lid.

All the time the frost persisted we had a happy winter. Copsford gave me its last rich gift – Winter Glory. I lived in a fairyland, a dream land, in the palace of the Snow Queen. I was intoxicated with its beauty. Between my daily tasks of gathering fuel and bringing home supplies I spent long glorious hours wandering in the wonderland of the snow-decked woods. The cottage was my igloo, the dazzling countryside my Polar Regions. Everywhere cried out 'Come and see me,' and I went. I travelled across untrod wilderness, I floundered in the crevasses of the marsh, I tracked the polar rabbit, I followed the Arctic fox, otters were my walrus, bank voles my seals. I reached the Pole and back in a single day, and no Amundsen forestalled me. Floss was my sled dog, my husky, and many a bold and daring passage we undertook, she harnessed with no more than a word and I riding on the clumsy sleigh of my imagination.

Copsford roared with tremendous fires. I tried the small grate in the bedroom in order that my upper room might be more comfortable for sleeping. But what a draught, what a draw! I never saw any fire blaze away as that did. It must have been something to do with the great draught which I had first discovered when sweeping out the cottage, for this fire blew as if a blacksmith's bellows were pumping at full blast beneath it. It was impossible to damp it down. It consumed board and branch in a few minutes, and the grate was so small I could put nothing substantial on it, and I could not risk tumbling logs in the bedroom. It was impossible to go on with it, so I continued sleeping in my one and only chair by the furnace downstairs.

In February the frost broke. The wind slowly backed round the clock and one morning the snow was no longer crisp, the bricks in the scullery were wet, the milk was not frozen in the can, Floss's feet made wet marks when she ran in, the fire burnt abominably and the smoke flopped out into the room, and I felt damp and cold and depressed with a sense of foreboding. By the afternoon it was raining, the skies were ragged grey, the wind was rising. By nightfall a veritable tempest burst upon Copsford. The palace of the Snow Queen dissolved and left not a wrack behind.

It was an appalling night. In all my ten months in the cottage I had never experienced half such frightful conditions. The lashing fury of the rain and the thunderous roar of the gale made neither rest nor sleep possible. Every moment I expected the shaky window frames to be blown in or the roof to be stripped off. As it was, the frost must have prised many an old crack, or burst new ones, for the cottage was leaking like a sieve and some slates certainly were torn off on the weather corner. Water poured into Copsford. It was not merely discoloured patches, or drips or trickles, the water literally did pour in, in several places at once. I could keep nothing dry, neither clothes nor bedclothes, nor chair nor food, nor matches nor myself.

By dawn I was beaten. Copsford was impossible. The writing on the wall had been plain to see; the music mistress had interpreted it aright long before, and now I knew. I was leaving. It was no place for man and woman to live.

Except for a few papers there was nothing to pack. Bed and bedding would remain maybe for weeks, or years. There was nothing among my oddments worth carrying away there and then; indeed I had not the wherewithal with which to transport them had I wished. So after a miserable cup of cold milk and some wet bread I whistled Floss and we walked out of Copsford.

It was over. I was glad and very sad. All the trials and tribulations, the loneliness, the dreariness, the stark wretchedness of that derelict, desolate, inhospitable, mean little building were finished with. I had triumphed, but had been beaten at the post. It had defied me, it had endured me, it now drove me out without so much as a stool under my arm. Drove me out into the wind and the rain as empty-handed as I had first come. I had nothing but the sodden clothes in which I stood. Nothing? Ah, indeed, I had everything! Clivers had twined a sweetheart round my heart. Foxglove had brought me freedom and centaury the fragrance of the countryside. Agrimony had skinned my fingers and given me a new sense of touch. *Clematis vitalba* had brought me traveller's joy. I had discovered a new world following along the scented trail of meadowsweet and tansy. Eyebright had washed my eyes that I might catch the glimpse of a kingdom. Yarrow brought me to mother earth and sweet chestnut showed me the hearts of men. Copsford, that mean little cottage, untenanted for twenty years, rat-ridden, rain-sodden, had been the talisman. I went out into the rain and heard behind me once again the forlorn rattle of ill-fitting windows and the sullen damp of its unlatched door. It was over.

Not quite. Copsford was not quite satisfied yet.

As I made my way through the driving rain, slipping and stumbling on the still-frozen ground, I suddenly beheld an amazing sight. The levels beside the Darn and its little tributary were two broad rivers joining in a mad whirl below Copsford. I stared at this bewildering sight, thinking I must be crazy. But it was real enough, as Floss and I found when we stood on the shores of the broad muddy flood. Marooned! Marooned on the little hill with only the leaking cottage as a shelter. More impossible than the impossible. It could not be.

I stripped on the shores of the flood. Holding my clothes in a bundle before me, I waded out into the icy, racing waters. I found the barred bridge and somehow crossed it. The water was breast-high on the other side and I had difficulty in keeping my feet, but at last I was across. I wedged my clothes in a bush and returned for Floss. Somehow we crossed the frothing waters at the bridge and then Floss swam the rest.

I stood, a naked man, in the midst of the floods; leaves, mud, froth, ice, swirled past me. I looked up to the hill through the streaming rain and could just see the top of that grey chimney. Copsford was peeping and satisfied.

The music mistress was awaiting me on the other side – not literally – and it was not long before we had a watertight roof over our heads, and Floss lies contented on the hearth rug, and the music mistress plays my pen to a standstill.

Little Toller Books

W. littletoller.co.uk   E. books@littletoller.co.uk